How Changeable Are You . . .

and How Can You Improve Your Ability to Change?

CQ

The Changeability Quotient

Norman Goldwasser, Ph.D.

Published by
Horizon Psychological Services
MIAMI BEACH, FLORIDA

ISBN: Softcover: 979-8-218-75568-3
        Hardcover: 979-8-218-75568-3

Cover and Interior: Gary A. Rosenberg • www.thebookcouple.com
Editing: Erica Meyer Rauzin

Printed in the United States of America

Contents

SECTION III **Issues Related to CQ**

SECTION IV **Final Thoughts**

Introduction

Change is a fundamental quality of being human. We're all in a constant state of flow, looking to change or improve our careers, our financial status, our health, our spirituality, or our relationships. We are not static beings, but rather we exist within a perpetual dynamic. Psychologists and other mental health professionals are universally overloaded with patients and clients who face challenges that require them to change in order to improve their outcomes or achieve important goals.

Over the last 30 years of practice, I have had the opportunity to develop an informal awareness of what makes one person more changeable—more able to change the way he or she is—than the next. Quite often, I have an intuitive sense about someone whom I think may be more workable than others, which can, in turn, predict a heightened ability to change. Many clinicians have this sense of who is going to be more successful. On the other hand, our ability to predict can be quite limited. Some patients whom I thought would be relatively easy to work with and successful turned out to be the "patients from hell," whereas others whom I thought would be impossible to work with ended up being tremendous success stories.

Psychologists in general are trained to interpret and analyze the past, as well as observe and measure the present, and, I think, we do a rather satisfactory job of that. However, we are notoriously poor at predicting the future. Even though some predictor factors can help us in this challenging endeavor, we are not prophets and can't readily predict what will happen down the road.

This book is an attempt to identify factors that can contribute to changeability and explore ways that people can improve their ability to change. Many of us, if not most of us, desire real change, but we may face factors that could hold us back. This is an attempt to assist those people who desire real change in identifying which traits they have that are strengths for them, and which traits they need to work on to improve their chances of being successful in the areas that they wish to change.

This is dedicated to the thousands of patients I have seen during the span of my career who have shown the grit and determination to change their lives for the better and to achieve important goals to improve their lives. I will be forever indebted to them for all I have learned from them and for the immense gratification that I experienced from watching them transform themselves into the people they wished to become. You are all truly a source of great inspiration.

SECTION I

The Concept of Changeability

"The only constant in life is change."

—HERACLITUS

CHAPTER 1

What Is Change?

Definitions

The Merriam-Webster dictionary defines the word "change" in several ways. These two definitions probably best describe the change that we are discussing:

1. To become different.

2. To undergo transformation or transition.

So, let's look at what these definitions mean, in terms of changeability. When we think about the need to change, in many ways we are saying that we have to make things different. It could be as simple as needing to change our wardrobe, change our diet, or alter our daily routine, or it could represent a more fundamental process of change. It could be that we must change in order for our situation to be different or, alternatively, that we have to change ourselves to become literally different people. This could mean becoming different in terms of the way we think, the way we act, or the way that we live our lives.

The second definition seems to represent more of a transformation of ourselves, rather than a behavioral transition. So, let's look at the difference between transition and transformation. Transitioning is a gradual evolution to becoming different. It happens over time, gradually, and in ways that are more subtle and less dramatic. Merriam-Webster defines it as, "the process or a period of changing from one state or condition to another." So, in this context, the emphasis is on a gradual process that involves change over time.

A transformation, on the other hand, is a more dramatic way of becoming a completely different person. Using the dictionary again, it defines transformation as, "a thorough or dramatic change in form or appearance." So, according to this definition, transformative change requires a major overhaul in how we think, how we behave, and how we function in our day-to-day lives over different situational contexts. For some people, transitioning from one discrete state of being to another is sufficient to achieve their goals. Others require a complete transformation to become the people they wish to be and for their lives to change in the direction they desire.

Within the context of our discussion, change doesn't happen just because a person recognizes the need to change. Different people change in different ways. They also change at different rates, and they vary in terms of the degree to which they are capable of achieving real change, whether it is the transitional type or more transformative change.

People also differ in the type of change that they are seeking. Some people see change in more limited ways. They want to change their diet or lose weight; they want to stop smoking or alter some other type of behavior. This level of change would require some type of limited, micro-level behavioral change. Not that this is easy, but it requires a limited focus and a very focused goal. Other examples of this type of change would be changing jobs or finding a different place to live. It requires some effort to come up with a plan, but this is still a limited, focused goal. People who come for therapy to achieve these kinds of goals often find that a behavioral therapy approach is most helpful because it focuses on a defined goal that requires specific steps to achieve. They are not looking for transformative change; rather they want to work on one specific problem that they feel needs to change.

Other people come into therapy for a more profound, transformative change that requires a far greater degree of sustained effort, motivation, and introspection. They aren't looking to change just one aspect of their lives; they are trying to change their entire way of living and being. They want to become literally different people in the way they think, feel, and function in their day-to-day lives.

Transformative change requires a more substantive, comprehensive effort to overhaul our personhood and to become the person we really want to be. The need for this type of transformative change usually emanates from a more profound dissatisfaction with how we are functioning and a subsequent desire to achieve the kind of change that will literally transform how we think, feel, react, and experience our lives. People with personality disorders who have difficulty in all their relationships and whose thinking, emotions, or behaviors interfere with most aspects of their lives usually require a more transformative, macro-level of change. The end goal of such transformative change is to accomplish a higher degree of functioning in all areas and generally to be more satisfied with the life they are living.

CHAPTER 2

Normative Change: The "I, I, Is" of Change— Incremental, Inconsistent, Incomplete

Over the years I have been in practice as a psychologist, I have realized that normative change, the kind of change that we should realistically expect, and not what we would ideally like to achieve, is a rather slow and laborious process. Whether we are hoping someone else will change, or whether we are trying to change ourselves, we have to understand and accept certain realities, so that our expectations are within some degree of reality and not just what we hope to achieve.

So, I came up with a (hopefully) cute acronym to describe what I think is the normal process of change that we expect of ourselves or those in our lives whom we hope will change. It's called "I I I," which stands for:

Incremental   Inconsistent   Incomplete

Incremental

We are all familiar with the term "one baby step at a time." That is what incremental means. We rarely change in "one fell swoop" and then suddenly achieve our goals or become a different person. Rather, change usually requires patience, both for the person who is carrying out the change and for those in his or her life. It's important to understand that change takes time.

What is even more important to understand is that—for all those involved (especially the therapist)—every step along the way, no matter how small or seemingly unimportant, should be reinforced. We should meet any evidence of change, whether relatively small or a concerted effort to change, with praise and encouragement. Many people whose personalities and behaviors require change to improve their relationships were damaged by critical, abusive parents or were bullied when younger. Often, they never received any positive feedback about themselves or their accomplishments, so being praised for small increments of change can inspire them to keep working at it and can help sustain their efforts to improve themselves. Conversely, if these small steps in the right direction are not recognized or, worse yet, are belittled or otherwise minimized, it could demotivate a person, and lead him or her to stop trying.

Remember that "Rome wasn't built in a day," and that real, sustainable change doesn't happen overnight either. Reasonable, realistic expectations are essential to ensure that you don't give up on yourself or others in your life when you—or they—don't achieve goals as quickly as you had expected.

Finally, I like to look at the process of transformation from "what I am" to "what I want to be" as a marathon, not a sprint. It often takes a long time, and continued efforts to celebrate the small victories along the way can keep you from being frustrated that you haven't reached your goals yet. In this regard, patience is certainly a virtue, and the ability to acknowledge your micro-achievements during your journey toward what you are trying to accomplish is as important as the ability to feel successful when you finally reach your goals.

Inconsistent

I am sure that you've heard the familiar adage, "Two steps forward, one step back." This saying is emblematic of the fact that real change isn't always linear, meaning that it isn't usually smooth sailing in the desired direction. Rather, more commonly, people start to show improvements toward their designated goal, and then they, on occasion, slip back into familiar patterns of undesirable behaviors or reactions. In addiction terms, this is called a lapse. Notice that there is a difference between a lapse and a full relapse, which is when people slip back into the baseline pattern of acting out that was evident before they decided to work on themselves. A lapse is a momentary step backward or a "slip" that doesn't have to mean that you have reverted completely back to your old ways.

If (or when) that happens, you shouldn't be discouraged or beat yourself up for failing in your efforts to change. This inconsistency in behavior is entirely normal, and you could see it as an opportunity to examine what went wrong that caused the slip, to learn the lesson to not repeat the mistake, and to develop a corrective action plan to prevent or minimize the probability that it will happen again.

Expecting that everything will go completely smoothly in your mission to change yourself is never realistic. It's always wiser to anticipate those steps backward. When they happen, hold on to this perspective, embrace the imperfections that come along with being human, and focus forward on being determined to not let it happen again.

This idea of inconsistency, being a normal and reality-based element of change, is especially important for partners or other loved ones to understand so that they don't get frustrated or demoralized when a slip occurs. Instead, it's essential to give support when these steps backward occur, to encourage people that it's okay to have momentary slips, and to emphasize how important it is to get back on track as quickly as possible, so as not to lose what they have achieved or their momentum for change.

Don't give in to the common need to expect perfection in your efforts to change or recover from addiction. In 12-step terms, "It's progress, not perfection, that counts." Perfectionists have difficulty tolerating mistakes and often fall into the trap of black-and-white thinking. They may feel that they have failed in their recovery or effort to change, just because they had a slip of some kind. People with Obsessive Compulsive Personality Disorder (OCPD) often exhibit these perfectionistic tendencies and have difficulty looking at the big picture—that these slips are normal and even expected.

Slips can also teach us a lot, in terms of what we need to look at and improve as we move forward. Remember, to be human is to be imperfect. We just have to do the best we can and keep on going, even if we fall back at times.

Incomplete

In all probability, whatever is challenging you is something that you'll have to, at least, be aware of, or keep working on for the rest of your life. Deep-seated personality traits, behavioral patterns, and addictive behaviors are all a result of neural pathways that have developed in your brain which cause you to reflexively revert to old patterns of reacting. Psychotherapy, treatment programs, 12-step programs, therapy groups, and other activities that promote meaningful change can all be effective in modifying these neural pathways and creating new, more adaptive neural pathways that result from these experiences. This can lead to real, substantive change.

But these pathways aren't always completely eradicated, and there may be instances when you have been in a new pattern of functioning for a long period and feel confident that the "new you" is here to stay. Please don't lull yourself into a false sense of security that you have no possibility of backsliding. Sustained, stable change requires an ongoing effort to stay vigilant about your behavioral reactions and thought patterns, remembering that lapses are always possible, even years into your efforts to work on yourself.

That doesn't necessarily mean that you have to be in intense therapy your entire life or that you must maintain the same level of intensity in your recovery program indefinitely, although some do feel the need for that. It just means that you "can't take your eye off the ball" over time and stop working on yourself just because you have accomplished your goals. Life should be about constant, ongoing efforts to learn, grow, and improve.

Some of the most inspiring people I have worked with over the years had been working on themselves for decades and had achieved most or all of their goals. Yet, they continued to read self-help books and to check in with me once in a while to keep working on their goals, or to develop and work on new goals. These growth-oriented individuals never allowed themselves to be complacent about what they had achieved or to lose focus on the need to continue to work on themselves. Rather, they see their lives as an ongoing evolution of themselves as dynamic, ever-changing people who never allowed themselves to be satisfied with the status quo. They are determined to reinforce their transformation in any way possible.

As an example, for more than 25 years, I have run a group for men who grew up in toxic, narcissistic homes and developed, in some cases, strong narcissistic traits or full-blown narcissistic personalities, and who fell into high-conflict relationships and/or addictions as a result. These brave men join together every week to share their stories and struggles, to hear each other's challenges and victories, and to use the experience to develop new perspectives about their lives and their relationships from a less narcissistic point of view.

Over the years, several men have stayed in the group well beyond the expected point. In fact, as of now, one gentleman has been in the group for close to 18 years and another for 14 years. They continue to come although they have accomplished all of their goals, and they are, at present, stable in their recovery from former addictions and successful in their efforts to remove the narcissism from their personalities and their relationships. Yet, they still come regularly, even after all this time. When asked why, they both respond by saying that they are fully aware that, even after all these years, they could slip back at any time, which they can ill afford.

By attending the group, they reinforce their changes by hearing new ways of thinking again and again and by reminding themselves of the importance of maintaining their new behavior patterns. More important, perhaps, they also see how much they gain by giving back what they received and helping others overcome their struggles. And finally, they benefit because being present helps them continue to strengthen and reinforce their efforts to sustain the changes they have achieved.

CASE STUDY #1: CHARLIE

Charlie is a 20-something medical student who has suffered from the legacy left by his unstable, drug-addicted mother who abandoned the family when he was seven years old. As a result, he is exquisitely sensitive to any form of abandonment, and he reacts strongly when people don't respond to his texts or don't include him in group activities. He especially overreacts to situations in which a woman breaks up with him and, as a result, he gets very emotionally destabilized. He has definite signs of OCD, which is common in people who were traumatized earlier in life. After his girlfriend broke up with him, his reactions were so extreme and unstable that he almost dropped out of medical school.

After working diligently on his early traumas through EMDR—a highly effective treatment that utilizes rapid eye movement to desensitize and reprocess trauma—Charlie was able to demonstrate gradual improvements in his ability to tolerate minor incidents of being ignored or excluded and to imagine being more stable in the event of future breakups. His improvements came in small increments over time as he grew better able to deal with situations that previously would derail him.

However, after Katie, a girl with whom he had a close relationship, informed him that she had met someone she had started dating, he had a strong negative reaction. He obsessed about Katie for months and couldn't accept the situation. His reaction and subsequent difficulty functioning weren't nearly as severe as the impact of his previous breakups, but it was still difficult for him. Over time, he recovered and was able to put the incident behind him, but he knows that he needs to be mindful about being prepared for similar incidents in the future.

Charlie's situation is a good example of how change is rarely like a light switch that you can just shut on and off. Rather, it comes in increments (Incremental), often with two steps forward and, at times, one step back (Inconsistent). It also demonstrates that trauma has a lasting effect; Charlie will probably be sensitive to the issue of abandonment throughout his life (Incomplete), although the lessons he learned in therapy should temper his reactions and make them less severe and more manageable.

CHAPTER 3

CQ: The Need for a Measure of Changeability

During the more than 30 years that I have been in practice, I realized over time—as noted in the introduction—that I had developed a sixth sense of sorts about patients I was seeing, specifically with regards to who I felt could change and who might be more of a challenge. In truth, earlier in my career, my predictive ability wasn't that great. Some of the people who came to see me who appeared at first to be dream clients—pleasant, motivated, and complimentary—ended up being tremendous challenges, and several people I thought that I had no chance of working with effectively ended up being huge success stories. Go figure. The truth is that psychologists are trained and able to analyze and explain the past, and we're usually effective in observing and measuring the present, but we are downright awful when it comes to predicting the future. Prophesy 101 wasn't offered in graduate school, much to my chagrin.

However, over time, I realized that patients may present predictor variables or factors that could help clinicians get a sense of who may be more likely to have the ability to change over time and achieve their goals, versus those who will find change more difficult, if not impossible to achieve. These factors were not subjected to or the result of any statistical analysis, mind you. Perhaps that will be my goal in my next life (statistics and I didn't exactly get along well while I was doing my doctoral training).

Still, I realized that identifying certain factors that could predict changeability would be helpful in several ways in a clinical practice. First, for the clinician, having a broad sense of a patient's potential for change could help create a realistic idea, in terms of prognosis, of how likely this person is to be able to make the changes necessary to reach his or her goals. Identifying specific factors that may be weak in this regard can lead to treatment goals, or at least to being able to define areas to be aware of within the context of therapy.

Assessing and identifying predictive factors can also help patients become aware of where they stand in terms of changeability, first by emphasizing areas of strength to encourage them about their ability to change. Then, it can be helpful toward the beginning of the therapy process to point out areas that they need to work on to enhance their ability to change and achieve their therapeutic goals. This can give them a sense of empowerment, in terms of their ability to succeed in therapy and, at the same time, help them understand and focus on areas they need to address that can help them achieve a more positive outcome.

Additionally, being able to derive a realistic assessment of a person's ability to change can be enormously helpful for the significant others in a patient's life. Quite often, when I am dealing with a patient's spouse or partner, I make sure to discuss the concept of changeability and, more specifically, my assessment of the patient's ability to change. In cases when the partner is negative or pessimistic about the chances that anything will change, I try to point out the areas of strength that could possibly help the person overcome the problems that are getting in the way of his or her relationships or attain the ability to function effectively, in general.

In situations in which the patient's expectations are unrealistic or unreasonable given the realities of their challenges, I point out the limitations and the extent of deficits that may make it difficult, if not unlikely, for change to happen. This can be important in situations in which family members insist on pushing a patient to achieve unattainable goals or to continue in therapy when clearly the process has come to its eventual conclusion due to the limitations or just the exhaustion of the unfortunate patient who truly lacks the ability to change further, if at all.

So, to identify, systematize, and empirically quantify the various factors that can predict a patient's ability to change, I realized the need to develop a method of evaluating changeability. So, similar to the concept of IQ, or Intelligence Quotient, and EQ, or Emotional Quotient, I thought of the idea of CQ, or Changeability Quotient. Just as IQ assesses one's intellectual abilities, and EQ measures one's emotional intelligence, CQ measures, at a macro level, one person's general ability to change, and at a micro level, it describes how people stack up on the different factors that shape their overall changeability.

CHAPTER 4

The Factors Included in the CQ

You may be thinking that the idea of a CQ actually makes some sense, in terms of the reasons discussed in the previous chapter. You may also wonder how I identified and ultimately selected the different factors to include in the CQ. As I alluded to earlier, I am a clinician, not a researcher, so developing statistical models and factor analyses to mathematically derive the most empirically valid factors to include in the CQ was beyond the purview of this effort. Perhaps I will leave that to some doctoral student to use in a future dissertation study. It actually would be helpful to conduct such a study, not only to empirically validate the selection of these factors, but also to analyze objectively the relative importance of these factors in predicting changeability. Perhaps those that weigh more heavily could become more of a focus in therapy, because concentrating on those factors could have a greater payoff than paying attention to factors that might be less important or less changeable.

The factors in the CQ are those that I have found over the years to be the most salient in determining an individual's ability to change. Initially, this awareness was actually rather subliminal and not the focus of my conscious awareness. Rather, it was more of a general realization that some patients were more able to change than others. Over time, my thinking coalesced into a more specific, conscious effort to isolate which factors seemed to influence changeability in these more successful patients. Eventually, I also became interested in what factors related to changeability actually impeded some more challenging patients from being able to benefit from therapy and kept them from achieving their therapeutic goals.

There was also a bit of an evolution in my thinking about the factors that I included in the CQ. Initially, I came up with six factors that I thought were the more obvious influencers of change, and I used those factors with patients for many years.

When I discussed CQ with them, either in terms of their own ability to change or the changeability of a loved one, I often asked them which factors they thought related to the ability to change. I was trying to get them to zero in on the half-dozen I had already identified. As my mentor in graduate school told me eons ago, "I learned more from my patients than from all my years in graduate school." How true. The lessons that I learned and the wisdom I gained from patients over the years are so valuable that they sometimes seemed to surpass what I gave them.

Based on actual suggestions from my patients, nine additional factors emerged as relevant determinants of the ability to change, for a total of fifteen factors.

These fifteen factors make up the CQ:

1. Motivated
2. Trusting
3. Workable
4. Intentional
5. Having integrity
6. Compliant
7. Stable
8. Introspective
9. Analytical
10. Flexible
11. Active
12. Disciplined
13. Optimistic
14. Inquisitive
15. Adequate support

We will discuss these factors at length in the coming chapters, but it is helpful for you to have an overview of the factors included in the CQ to see what exactly we are referring to when we refer to CQ and to analyze these factors generally to see commonalities and distinctions among them.

What becomes apparent is that, except for the last factor, they are all about you—or, more specifically, aspects of yourself that are required for change or will help facilitate change. This is important because many dependent or externally oriented people rely on others to help them change, or they put the responsibility for their ability to change onto other people in their lives. So, if you are serious about changing your life, or yourself, the obvious place to start is inside you, instead of reflexively looking to others to help you.

This doesn't preclude getting help to assist you in the process of change. It just means that, first, you have to get a good sense of how really changeable you are, what factors you have going for you that can positively influence your ability to change, and what factors can hold you back. Doing this self-assessment and taking the necessary measures to improve those areas of weakness, will greatly enhance your ability to change and the extent to which you'll succeed in meeting your goals.

These factors are predicated on the assumption that you want to change. We will discuss motivation at greater length in later chapters, but if there is one overarching factor that probably carries the greatest weight in predicting future change, it's motivation. As the old "shrink" joke goes,

Question: *"How many psychologists does it take to change a light bulb?"*

Answer: *"It depends on how much the light bulb wants to change."*

That's why I list motivation first: without it, change is unlikely, and that makes all of the other factors meaningless.

Finally, a lot of these factors relate to your general personality. So, if you're generally a thoughtful, open-minded, flexible person, who is also optimistic and generally stable, you are much more likely to achieve meaningful change than if you are not.

So, with that in mind, let's look at the factors that may limit your ability to change and could hold you back from progressing with your life, in general. And let's see what we can do about them.

CHAPTER 5

Factors that Limit
Changeability

Just as some factors can contribute to or predict changeability, some factors also can impede or reduce someone's
ability to change. This is a meaningful part of our discussion
because it may be as important to identify what is holding
you back from changing as it is to understand what can help
enhance your ability to change.

The limiting factors that I have identified over the years
also are not the result of any factor analysis per se but are
characteristics that make a patient's progress in therapy more
difficult, if not impossible. They all seem to coalesce around
the theme of impediments to progress toward meaningful
change. Similarly, the ordering of these factors reflects a
general listing in terms of factors that limit changeability, as
opposed to the order of their severity or the seriousness of the
challenge. The truth is that—unless you address these factors
systematically—any one of them can easily keep you from
being able to accomplish the change you want.

Limiting Factors

1. Sabotaging	6. Resistant	11. Passive
2. Distrustful	7. Unstable	12. Uncontrolled
3. Difficult	8. Blocked	13. Pessimistic
4. Clueless	9. Concrete	14. Defensive
5. Dishonest	10. Rigid	15. Doing it Alone

As you may be able to see, these impediments correspond directly to the 15 factors that are included in the CQ and were delineated in the last chapter. Those CQ factors describe ways in which your changeability can be enhanced, whereas these impediments specify what will hold you back from changing.

Similar to the positive factors, all but one of these factors involves something about the person seeking change, whereas the last factor is external since it concerns the amount of support someone has. So, the bad news is that, if you can identify with any of these first 14 factors, you're a big part of the problem. The good news is that you can also be a big part of the solution.

The key here is being able to engage in some honest self-reflection, to take a good, unfiltered look at these factors, and to ask yourself, "Which of these do I identify with and what am I willing to do about it?" This type of honest self-assessment is vital to being able to change the things you want to work on about yourself because, without this step in the process, you're likely to be held back by the very issues that you're being asked to identify and tackle.

Facing your flaws is often uncomfortable, even threatening, especially when it comes to factors that are not easy to admit about yourself. Yet, it can be freeing to face the reality of your situation and to be able finally to identify the things that may have been keeping you from making the changes in your life that you have known you need for quite some time. Taking a good look at this list can be the catalyst for the change that you have been seeking throughout your life. Embracing this as an opportunity for honest self-appraisal and then removing the roadblocks to your personal recovery can be quite liberating—but only if you're willing to take an honest look at yourself and identify which of these limiting factors may be getting in the way of your progress toward real change.

You may also want to consider allowing your significant other, a friend, or a family member to go over the list and give you some honest feedback about how they see you with regard to these limiting factors. Sometimes, we are the last to realize (or admit) painful truths about ourselves, because it is often so hard to be this brutally honest with ourselves. Often, our defenses get in the way, and we place the blame on others, or we prefer to focus on the flaws of the people around us instead of facing what's gone wrong with ourselves.

This is especially true about people with narcissistic traits who find it particularly difficult to face their flaws and often project them onto others. These people usually have weak cores, and they find it difficult to face their flaws because it is so threatening to their fragile egos. Still, it's vital to identify the factors that are holding them back if they are ever going to change successfully. Being able to stay in reality, then, is imperative to achieving meaningful change.

That trusted person can be the valuable source of vital, objective information you need to get on a good track. Having someone you trust to be honest and accurate about you, someone who cares enough about you to be totally candid can be exactly what you need to get headed in the right direction.

As a therapist, I was trained in the tradition of Harry Stack Sullivan, who developed the concept of Interpersonal Communication Therapy. My mentor taught me to give patients honest feedback about how they are affecting me, because it is likely that this is how they are impacting the other people in their lives, as well. Many, if not most, conscientious patients actually appreciate and recognize the value of such feedback, because it is likely that they would never otherwise receive that kind of useful transparency and honesty from anyone else.

If you make the effort to ask someone you trust for honest feedback regarding the limiting factors that may be inhibiting your ability to change, you may be surprised how willing he or she may be to respond to your request once it's clear that you are sincere about wanting the feedback. Of course, you'll need to be explicit about the fact that you do want the feedback and that you won't hold it against them if they are totally honest with you. It is also important to show them appreciation for taking the risk of being honest with you and to tell them how valuable the information is to you in enabling you to work on yourself effectively.

So, now that we have identified the positive factors that predict changeability (CQ), as well as the limiting factors that can inhibit the ability to change and reduce CQ, let's review these factors in greater detail.

The Specific Factors Included in CQ and Their Corresponding Limiting Factors

"The measure of intelligence
is the ability to change."

—ALBERT EINSTEIN

CHAPTER 6

FACTOR ONE:
Motivated vs. Sabotaging

Motivated

At first glance, what comes to mind is that the first factor seems rather obvious. You're not going to change if you're not motivated. Or, to put it a bit differently, the amount of motivation that you have to change is directly correlated to the probability that you will change. None of the other factors will mean much if you're not motivated or ready to work on yourself.

So, if you're in therapy because:

A. Your spouse, parent, or child told you that you need help, but you're not intrinsically ready or accepting of that reality, or

B. You have convinced yourself that they have the problem, not you,

then, how motivated will you be to change? How willing will you be to work hard on yourself? Probably not very much.

So, the first thing you should deal with is to ask how really motivated you are. Do you have a genuine understanding and acceptance of the need to change, or are you just going through the motions? Changing yourself is hard enough if you are sincerely motivated and willing to work hard at it, but if you aren't truly motivated, you really don't have much chance of success.

Assessing your true motivation involves some honest reflection. Why are you in therapy or trying to work on yourself in the first place? Were you coerced, threatened, or shamed into going for help? Or did your decision to come to therapy result from a more mature realization that your problems in life won't go away unless you work on yourself? Honest self-reflection is absolutely vital in motivating yourself to change.

Mind you, being pushed or threatened isn't always a problem in terms of motivation. This is often referred to as "external" motivation, which basically means that the motivation came from forces outside of yourself. So, if your wife tells you that unless you get your anger under control or get a hold of your drinking, she is leaving you, that will certainly motivate you—at least, to a certain degree. Similarly, if your children haven't spoken to you for quite a while because of your propensity to have affairs, then you may be more likely to get help to remedy that estrangement. External motivation isn't necessarily a bad thing, and it can propel you forward to face the things about yourself that you don't want to face or don't have sufficient reasons to confront.

On the other hand, being motivated to change because you want to change, perhaps because you have the insight to understand that your life is not going the way you want it to, or because you realize that you are out of control, is called intrinsic motivation. Wanting to change for your own reasons, and not because you have a gun to your head, or because you're being coerced, is usually more powerful than being forced to change. You may wonder why this is so. Maybe an outside threat that demands change can be an even more powerful motivator than an internal desire in catalyzing the need to change.

In truth, being threatened or forced to change can be a strong motivator to get people to face their problems and commit to change. I have had many patients over the years who came into my office not of their own volition and were quite successful in their effort to change. However, it is also true that those whose motivation comes from within, who are truly sincere in their efforts to become the best that they can be for their own purposes and not to please others, often achieve change that is more sustainable and deeply rooted. This type of internally motivated change tends to be more lasting because the drive to be different comes from within the person, and that drive is more likely to continue, even if no one else is aware of it or cares.

An externally motivated person may work hard to save a marriage or reconnect with his or her children, but over time, and after the crisis has passed, may be more likely to revert to old patterns of behavior and lose the motivation to maintain the changes, because the reason for the motivation has diminished over time.

Nevertheless, motivation is still motivation, and some type of motivation, even if it's entirely external, is certainly better than none at all. So, what can you do if you know that you need to change somehow, but you're not motivated to change? Often, in therapy, I can create motivation externally by using what is called in behavioral psychology "contingency management." In general, this relates to the concept of "if... then." In other words, if a person steps up and takes on the challenge of working on him or herself, then he or she can earn rewards, such as being able to stay at home, keep a job, put off an impending divorce, have contact with children, and so on. This is positive reinforcement, in that the person is being reinforced for complying with treatment. However, the person must also understand that if he or she refuses to get help or comply with treatment requirements, then he or she will need to leave home, lose the job, face divorce proceedings, or be permanently cut off from the children.

This is a classic form of external motivation, which although not optimal, can still get a person sufficiently motivated to at least start the process and hopefully sustain the effort to change, whether to obtain the positive reinforcement or to avoid the negative consequences of failure.

Obviously, it's preferable for you to find the reasons inside of yourself to work on yourself, without having to resort to some type of positive or negative reinforcer, which less mature or less emotionally healthy individuals may need if they can't muster the desire to change on their own. You would certainly prefer for your motivation for change to be self-driven, so you are the master of your own destiny, as opposed to being at the mercy of others.

How do you develop internal motivation when you don't

have it? That's the $64,000 question. To illustrate, for the past year I have been working with a patient, Tom, who was separated from his wife. She had enough of his narcissistic, controlling behavior and constant criticism, which destroyed her self-esteem and her entire sense of self. He said to me, at first, that he realized that he had to get his act together if he wanted to get his marriage back on track and to have his wife back.

But it became apparent to her that he was only undergoing therapy to patch things up, and to get back into the house (external motivation). She realized that this wasn't going to work for her. For her to trust that whatever changes he made would last over time, she felt he had to make sure these changes came from within himself—an inner awareness that things need to change, not only for her, but for his own well-being (internal motivation).

This provided me with the opportunity to urge him to reflect about himself and to make a more genuine effort to step out of himself to realize what his behavior had done to his wife and to their relationship, and why she had wanted him out of the house in the first place. This forced him to be more introspective and to accept that his behavior would destroy any future relationships, because, over time, and after all his charm had worn off, no one would put up with the abuse. This enabled him to get beyond the external motivating goal of just getting back into the house, and to focus on the internal motivating goal of healing the wounds that had resulted in his narcissism, and to learn the art of humility, compassion, and respect.

This reflects an approach in therapy called "motivational interviewing" that focuses on ways to catalyze motivation by exploring how therapy can enhance your life, improve your relationships, and help you achieve important goals. It can be an important first step in the process that can measurably improve the chances of achieving a positive outcome.

To sum up, motivation is vital for any real change. Whether the motivation is external or internal, some sort of motivation is required for a person to make the effort and do the work needed for real change. So, before you set out with the goal of changing yourself, you may want to check the level of motivation that you are feeling and ask whether it is coming from external sources or from within yourself. It may be helpful, if not required, to see what you can do to upgrade the amount of motivation you are experiencing and to try to work on making it more internal, from within yourself, before embarking on the journey of self-transformation.

CASE STUDY #2: MICHELLE

A single mother in her 30s who has been divorced for over a year, Michelle had been struggling with alcohol abuse for many years. Her divorce occurred largely as a result of her drinking and her inability (or unwillingness) to commit to dealing with her problem. She was to a great extent in denial about how it had affected her life and that of her 11-year-old daughter, Nikki.

She arrived for treatment the day after her family met with her for an intervention. She was shocked that they had forcefully challenged her to get the help that she desperately needed. They feared that if she didn't get a grip on her alcohol problem, Child Protective Services could remove Nikki from her home. They warned her that if a neighbor observed her drunkenness, and reported her, she could lose her child.

Although Michelle didn't feel that her drinking was such a big deal, she realized that her behavior could lead to serious trouble and that she needed to get her act together. She entered treatment with some resentment about being forced to work on herself.

However, over time, she came to realize that she had been drinking to escape from the pain of the sexual abuse that she had experienced at age 12 at the hands of a once-trusted uncle. Once she realized that this was the core of the issue and that she clearly had to deal with it, she was able to shift from the external motivators of her family's pressure and threats, and toward the internal motivation that came from facing the difficult reality that she had been traumatized in early adolescence.

Michelle came to understand that her drinking was an effort, albeit maladaptive, to numb the pain of her abuse. She finally was able to grasp how important it was for her and her daughter for her to get the help she needed to clear the trauma of the past and gain control of her dangerous behavior. Motivated now by self-understanding and the desire to carve a good future for herself and Nikki, Michelle embraced therapy and made good progress.

Sabotaging

So, now that we have explored the need for motivation as a factor in CQ, let's look at the limiting factor that corresponds to motivation, which is sabotage. Essentially, this involves consciously or subconsciously making sure that efforts to get you to change will fail. In that sense, it's the opposite of motivation, in that it actually reduces, or even eliminates the chances that change will occur, whereas motivation increases the probability of change.

People sabotage therapy, or other efforts to get them to change, for a variety of reasons. Probably the most common reason is that they are being forced to change and, instead of actively resisting these efforts, they become passive-aggressive and resist in more subtle, passive ways. Not complying with recommendations or homework is probably the most common form of this type of sabotage. Many patients I have seen over the years really didn't want to be in therapy, and they showed it with this type of passive non-compliance. Sometimes, when I called them on it, they acknowledged that they were fully aware of what they were doing. Other times, however, they were not aware or conscious of what was happening until I raised the possibility that their actions stem from their unconscious effort to sabotage treatment or to show their resentment about having to be in therapy in the first place.

Other examples of sabotage include habitually coming late, missing, forgetting (or pretending to forget) appointments, or canceling at the last minute with some sort of excuse that could have been avoided. Not only does this make any progress impossible, but it also often ends up alienating the therapist and sabotaging whatever therapeutic relationship had been previously developed. Often, the necessary therapeutic alliance never develops in the first place because of the patient's efforts—conscious or otherwise—to sabotage what could have been a healthy, helping relationship.

Another reason that people sabotage their loved one's efforts to get them to work on themselves is the perception that they are being controlled. People with narcissistic personalities are especially sensitive about being controlled because it makes them feel vulnerable and out of control. They also feel criticized unjustly for their way of thinking, so they often try to deflect the feedback by gaslighting or shifting the focus to the reactions of their significant others, rather than accepting responsibility for what they are doing to provoke and damage their relationships. So, instead of owning the problem, and motivating themselves to change, they use the false narrative of control, or of how wounded they are by criticism, to justify sabotaging sincere efforts to get them to work on the changes needed to save their relationships.

Sabotage also occurs for other, more complex reasons. Quite often, people who were abused or neglected in their earlier, formative years internalize a message of worthlessness and lack of value as a person. At a subconscious level, they come to feel that they are not worthy of being loved or having a loving relationship. Sadly, they submit to early programming that communicated to them, either implicitly or explicitly, that they are unworthy of being loved and intrinsically unlovable.

So, they unconsciously sabotage relationships that could lead to feeling loved, because they deem themselves unworthy or they convince themselves that they ultimately will be rejected once it becomes apparent how truly unlovable and worthless they really are.

Similarly, people who end up in therapy, even of their own volition, can often sabotage the therapeutic process because of this dynamic, which is beyond their conscious awareness. They are literally unaware that they are doing things to make change difficult or complicated in order to sabotage the process. That's why it's so important for an astute therapist to bring these unconscious dynamics to the level of the patient's conscious awareness so that the person can be more aware of what's really happening and can take the necessary measures to stop the sabotage. I have found that patients can often turn things around once they become aware of this dynamic, especially when they've already done some work to alter the distorted self-perception of being worthless or not having any value.

Regardless of the reasons for the sabotage, it is imperative to face and confront it if there is to be any hope of change. Those who are unaware of this sabotage dynamic will probably have the easiest time turning things around, especially after doing the work to challenge the false narratives underlying their sabotage.

Once you come to realize and accept that you are indeed quite worthy and lovable, and that your parents, or the other people who were abusive toward you, were really the problem (and not you), then you can then make a conscious effort to reverse your efforts to sabotage change and attain the motivation you need to accomplish your goals.

Unfortunately, it may be a bit more challenging to turn around your conscious or deliberate efforts to sabotage change. If you are doing these actions knowingly, then you are making deliberate choices that will impede you from improving your relationships and your life in general. Having the people in your life unhappy with you and constantly complaining about your behavior can't be a lot of fun, to say the least. Therefore, it makes sense to reevaluate your choices and to make better decisions about how you approach efforts to help you to change, whether they come from your family, friends, or a therapist.

Ultimately, we all have to make sense of our own choices. If what we decide to do backfires in terms of the outcome, then maybe we need to reevaluate those choices and, perhaps, choose instead to stop sabotaging the efforts of the people who genuinely care enough about us to try to save us from our own self-destructive behaviors.

Ultimately, the choices we make determine the outcomes in our lives.

CASE STUDY #3: JOELLE

Joelle, a 37-year-old woman with a history of multiple failed attempts at individual and marital therapy, came in with her husband Marcus to work on their marriage, which had been frustrating and difficult for both of them. They had been married for more than 10 years and had two young children, but their relationship had been challenging from the start. They both admitted that, at the beginning, their attraction was primarily physical, and that the attraction began to wane fairly quickly after they got married because of their constant fighting.

Marcus expressed extreme resentment about the daily criticisms Joelle leveled at him. As someone with ADHD, he is particularly sensitive to criticism. He said she had become controlling and emasculating. Joelle complained that her husband was completely incapable of showing her any love or respect. She went on to describe a litany of his faults in exhausting detail.

It became clear to me early on that she has Obsessive Compulsive Personality Disorder (OCPD), which usually shows up as being perfectionistic, highly critical, extremely defensive, with black-and-white thinking, and unrealistically high expectations. OCPD is different from OCD in that OCD is a mental illness characterized by obsessive thinking and compulsive behaviors that are beyond the person's control, but which can be very distressing to the person. On the other hand, OCPD is a personality disorder that a person can be very comfortable with and is therefore less likely to change. The two conditions have some overlapping symptoms, but they are very different.

Marcus could do very little that was right in Joelle's eyes, and as a result, he had shut down long ago and had withdrawn from her. He had given up any hope that he could ever get through to her and get her to see how damaging her behavior was to their relationship.

When I attempted to engage Joelle in trying to be more introspective in order to help her see that, just possibly, she was contributing to their troubled dynamic, she became entrenched in her conviction that Marcus was the problem and that I just "didn't get it." She met all my efforts to get her to see past her own narrative and to understand her husband's perspective with scorn and resistance. When I pointed out to her that she was the one who came for help and who didn't want to get divorced, she said she was there to do the work. Yet, when it came to following through with any therapeutic recommendations, she didn't make any attempt to change her behavior or attitude. She only wanted to continue obsessively going over, in excruciating detail, all of her husband's missteps and failings and to continue her litany about how much she was suffering as a result.

It was true that she was a hardworking, conscientious person, and that he didn't show much appreciation for her hard work, but she wouldn't, or couldn't, take any responsibility for the fact that her personality had caused complete alienation in the marriage and had pushed an otherwise potentially loving husband to be distant and resentful.

Her rigid, defensive, critical personality sabotaged all efforts to help the couple work toward the goal of having a healthier, more functional relationship. A month after she terminated therapy because, as she put it, "We were going nowhere, and that Dr. G, he was the worst..." Marcus filed for divorce. He called me and said that he felt he had no choice. I had been his last hope, and Joelle's defensiveness and rigidity had sabotaged every therapy that they had ever tried, including this one.

CHAPTER 7

Factor Two:
Trusting vs. Mistrustful

Trust

Next to motivation, the ability to trust another person, more specifically, a concerned significant other or a therapist, could be the single most important factor in determining your changeability.

This also should seem obvious because to be convinced that you need to change and can change, you have to trust the person giving you that feedback. If you can view other people in your life as well-intentioned and trustworthy, then you are more likely to accept their message about what you need to change with an open mind and a trusting heart. If you believe their feedback comes from genuine concern and caring, you are more apt to take some action toward change.

Even if the people who are giving you feedback are being emotional or harsh, they aren't necessarily trying to harm you. They may just be triggered and reacting to something you have done that reflects a problem you need to change. Their passion doesn't make what they're saying any less valid or important.

Don't allow yourself to gaslight and project the blame onto them by focusing on their reactions to your behavior, instead of paying attention to your behavior itself. Try to trust that they are expressing genuine emotions, even if their reaction seems extreme or hurtful. Try to accept that it reflects something you need to change.

Once you (hopefully) trust the feedback enough to decide to get help or you are forced by to get help the risk of losing an important relationship or a job, then your ability to trust is crucial to developing a therapeutic relationship with your therapist. Trusting that your therapist is there to help you and has only your best interests at heart will greatly expedite the therapeutic process, and it will help you avoid the painful and costly delays that can result from trust issues. Even if you have trust issues in general, trying to overcome them so you can achieve a positive outcome in therapy will greatly enhance your ability to change and, thereby, will give you a higher CQ.

That doesn't mean that your feeling that you might not be able to completely trust your therapist stems automatically from your trust issues. It is possible that the therapist has done something to legitimately compromise your trust, like violate your boundaries or break confidentiality. Perhaps something happened that caused you to question the therapist's competence or qualifications, and therefore, led you to lose trust in the therapist. These are all valid reasons to lose trust, but they don't mean that you can't trust another therapist or the therapy process. It just means you may have to do more due diligence to find the right therapist. Ask more people to recommend a therapist you can come to trust. Remember, "one bad apple doesn't spoil the whole bunch..."

Mistrust

Some people have difficulty trusting, in general. Their mistrust may be their general disposition toward everyone or just part of their personality structure.

People have issues involving trust for a number of reasons. Quite often, people who experience "betrayal traumas" end up having issues with mistrust. These are traumas involving people who are close to you, a parent, a teacher, a spouse, a friend or a sibling, who do something so traumatic that it causes a severe betrayal of trust that ends up generalizing to all your relationships or all the people in your life.

People who have been emotionally or sexually abused, abandoned by a parent, or severely bullied by classmates often end up with serious problems trusting others later in life. These people can have difficulties forming a trusting relationship. If they do end up in a committed relationship, they often can feel unable to trust their partner or whatever the partner says. These people obviously will also often have difficulty trusting their therapist, because, at least at an unconscious level, they expect the therapist will also betray their trust. It is difficult to imagine that you can expect any real personal change under these circumstances.

Paranoia is another clinical issue that can make the ability to trust difficult, if not impossible. This is a clinical disorder in which the person's mistrust is of such magnitude that it is delusional, almost to the point of being psychotic. Paranoid people, as a rule, distort reality and assume that people are "out to get them." They may believe in untenable conspiracy theories. Extreme cases are fairly rare and are often associated with schizophrenia or other forms of psychosis. More often, people have paranoid personalities, which are basically untrusting, suspicious, and guarded. Obviously, these people are generally not good candidates for psychotherapy, because they cannot allow themselves to trust the therapist or the process. Their CQ, therefore, is usually quite low as a result.

CASE STUDY #4: LINDA

An attractive, single redhead with piercing green eyes, Linda makes a striking first impression, but behind the façade of her beautiful appearance lay a disturbed personality that had prominent paranoid features. A friend had referred her to me, and she asked if I would take her on as a patient. She was a victim of incest, in the form of years of sexual abuse by her father. As a result, her ability to trust anyone, especially a man, was severely affected.

She initially presented as a guarded, hesitant person, who was quite ambivalent about trying therapy. She had heard about EMDR from her friend, who described it as the gold standard for trauma, and she decided to try it. She knew that her traumatic childhood had affected her deeply, and she realized that the time had come to do something about it.

When she shared her history with me during our first session, it became readily apparent that her ability to trust was compromised. I asked her if she felt that she would feel more comfortable and safer with a female therapist. She immediately accused me of trying to "dump her" because she was too much to handle. When I gently tried to explain that I was just making a suggestion given her betrayal traumas from her father's abuse, she became convinced that I was trying to wiggle out of the situation by explaining away my real intention to get rid of her as a patient. It was a rough start, to say the least.

(It's times like this when I wonder why I didn't choose to do something less challenging, like... accounting. Then I realize what kind of accountant I would make, and that reminds me why I'm not an accountant...)

In any case, her therapy was a difficult ride for both of us since she could not overcome her deeply rooted mistrust. Unfortunately, she derailed therapy several times because of an imagined (or actual) misstep on my part. Each incident became an entire drama and yet another reason why I was not worthy of her trust. This made any real progress quite difficult, as you can imagine.

It took quite a while to get her to trust me enough even to try EMDR, but after a few false starts, she was able to let go of her resistance, and allow the process to unfold and do its magic. After an intense, but highly stress-relieving session in which she was able to face her traumas, we could move ahead. As she became able to trust me just enough to complete the EMDR process, she eventually desensitized and reprocessed her trauma.

Linda began the slow road to recovery without letting her paranoia get in the way of her ability to make progress. Yet, the ongoing emergence of her paranoia complicated her therapy considerably and compromised her capacity to change enough to achieve her primary goal of being able to attain and maintain a healthy, trusting relationship.

Despite her successful EMDR, and a general reduction in her trauma symptoms, she was never able to overcome her mistrust of me and the entire profession of psychology. Linda eventually stopped therapy rather abruptly after she became convinced that I had been late for a session because I was deliberately trying to antagonize her. I never heard from her again, but I hope that she is making progress with another therapist.

CHAPTER 8

FACTOR THREE: Workable vs. Difficult

Workable

The concept of workability is closely related to changeability. It measures how workable a person is, or to put it another way, how easy it is for a therapist to work with a particular person. In my experience, workability is highly correlated with changeability because people who are easier to work with are more likely to put forth the effort that is necessary for change. It's really that simple.

So, what constitutes workability? People who show up on time and are determined to change and to do whatever is necessary to achieve what they set out to accomplish, are often considered workable. They are easy to relate to; they try to be pleasant and follow through on whatever they commit to doing. Highly workable people are collaborative and cooperative. They see themselves as active partners in the change process. They don't just sit and wait passively for the therapist to tell them what to do. Instead, they come into a session with their own agendas of what they would like to work on or accomplish.

I also find that more workable patients take notes at our sessions, and more importantly, they review the notes and refer back to them as needed. They ask questions if they don't fully understand something I have said because they truly want to make sure that they fully comprehend what we're discussing. They also comment rather frequently about things I say, because they want to contribute actively to the discussion. This shows that the material we're discussing really matters to them and that they are working to become active participants in the process.

I find that more workable people also tend to be more agreeable and lighthearted and to respond to my attempts at being humorous. They enjoy the experience of therapy and find it stimulating and rewarding. In addition, more workable people are often patient and realistic in terms of what it actually takes—and how long it takes—to see the results that lead to meaningful change.

Finally, people who come into therapy with clear goals and who know what they want or need to accomplish are usually more workable than those who sit there with no clue. When you ask them, "So, tell me, why are you here?", they often shrug their shoulders and respond with something like, "I don't know" or "No idea."

So, with that final, exhilarating comment, let's pivot to discuss the other ways that people can be less than workable.

Difficult

People who are difficult to work with are generally unpleasant, negative, and argumentative. They often actively resist attempts to get them to take responsibility for their issues or behavior and the damage that they have caused.

People who are passive and don't take an active role in the therapeutic process also lack workability and can be considered difficult. They expect the therapist to shoulder the sole responsibility for each session and for the entire process of change. Nothing is more frustrating to a therapist than finding yourself working hard to engage someone, only to be met with stony silence and no meaningful response. Therapists find it challenging to feel that the entire burden of change is on them, without an active participant who sees the potential benefit and who acts to move the process forward. Although it is often reasonable to expect that we, as therapists, need to motivate and mobilize productive energy in our patients, it is still difficult, and it calls into question how workable the patient is really going to be.

Patients also can be passive-aggressive. Instead of expressing their feelings about the therapist or therapy in general, they express their feelings indirectly through passive means, such as skipping appointments, not following through on assignments, making sarcastic comments, or minimizing the importance of the work involved.

People who are not as workable as they need to be to succeed in changing also often don't seem to take the process as seriously as they should. They don't appreciate the work they need to do to accomplish challenging goals, and they are unwilling to make the effort to achieve their objectives, if they have any. Those who are forced to work on themselves by other people may resent the position they have been put into, which is likely to end up with them being not too workable.

I have found that people who want to work on themselves are serious about the challenges that the need to change often poses, and they come in with the right attitude. Patients with a real intent to change are workable enough to increase their chances of success significantly. That's precisely why workability is so highly correlated with CQ.

CASE STUDY #5: CAROLYN

Carolyn was a professional in her late 40s when she came in for treatment of severe depression that resulted from her husband George leaving her, with no notice, to live with her friend, Lucy, who also happened to be his administrative assistant. He had been having an affair with Lucy for several years, unbeknownst to Carolyn. The shock of him leaving her, along with the trauma of finding out that her trusted friend had betrayed her, caused Carolyn to shut down emotionally. As a result, she had to take a leave of absence from her position as a dean of a local college.

One complicating factor was that she had underlying traits of Obsessive-Compulsive Personality Disorder (OCPD), which, in some ways, has been adaptive for her. She is an organized, highly competent person. Her strong need for things to be structured, predictable, and in order helped her achieve a successful career.

The trauma of her husband's betrayal had derailed her and caused a flurry of disturbing, maladaptive symptoms of OCD, in addition to her OCPD. These included endless ruminations about what happened, a compulsive need to review the details repeatedly with her friends, and a constant checking of George's credit card charges and social media accounts to track his whereabouts and to see what he was spending on Lucy. This had driven her to the point of utter exhaustion, which led her to reach out to me for help.

Carolyn was clearly in trouble. She was quite desperate to get some relief from her deep depression and intense OCD symptoms. The positive traits associated with her OCPD, however, helped me assist her more effectively. She was reliable, conscientious, and eager to work to reframe and get rid of her negativity and constant obsession with George.

She was open to trying anti-depressant medications, which, over time, helped her immensely. She voraciously read the books and articles that I recommended to her about trauma, EMDR, OCPD, and depression, and she actually enjoyed the exercises that I gave her.

After a short while, Carolyn was able to recognize her husband's narcissism and his controlling nature and to see that she was actually fortunate to be rid of someone who would never be capable of loving her or meeting any of her legitimate emotional needs. She realized that she had thrown herself into her educational and career goals to fill the empty void that resulted from her husband's self-centeredness and that his departure gave her an opportunity to get out of the marriage and find some happiness, either alone or in a healthier relationship. Her decision to initiate a divorce made her feel empowered and liberated.

Over time, Carolyn became more cheerful, and a humorous side came out, which made our conversations quite enjoyable. We transitioned from crisis intervention to crisis stabilization, and then to active recovery treatment, and finally toward goals of self-actualization and self-fulfillment. She decided that she was going to let go of the rigidity and conventionality of her former self and start a new life. She retired from her position at the college, started writing a book about her trauma and recovery, lost weight, and changed her look from that of a rather dowdy, grey-haired college dean to a blonde, colorful fashion plate. She told me she looked forward to each session when she could share her latest accomplishment in transforming herself.

Carolyn was an excellent example of someone who was highly workable. Motivated and compliant, she was willing to make the effort to change. She was internally energized to remake herself, to get beyond just recovering from her trauma, and to treat her depression. She took advantage of the opportunity offered by a positive therapeutic experience to transform her life into something that gave her great personal satisfaction and happiness compared to her previously colorless life.

For me, she was simply a joy to work with.

CHAPTER 9

FACTOR FOUR:
Intentional vs. Clueless

Intentional

I recently had an extraordinary experience, perhaps one of the most profound that I have ever had in my career as a psychologist, and it made me realize that I must discuss an issue that relates significantly to CQ.

In my work as a trauma psychologist, I have had quite a few patients who struggled with various types of addictions, including, drugs, alcohol, gambling, and sex. For the most part, the treatment formulas I use to help people heal from the psychological ravages of trauma and addiction are effective. Often, I can help them achieve recovery and stability. However, sometimes what I have to offer just isn't enough to get these patients to where they need to be, and they continue to suffer and struggle. As a therapist, the frustrating, humbling experience of failing requires me to come to terms with the understanding that psychologists and therapists are not omnipotent, and that we, too, can come up short in what we strive to do to help our patients.

Recently, I realized that several of my patients were just not progressing sufficiently in their recovery. They were still struggling greatly to overcome the effects of trauma, stabilize their emotional instabilities, and address and begin to repair the various ways that addictions were affecting their lives and their families.

One patient told me that he was interested in pursuing a psychedelic experience since a friend of his told him this had dramatically helped him. This friend stopped acting out immediately after having an intense therapeutic experience with psilocybin, or "magic mushrooms." I had discussed the concept of psychedelic-assisted psychotherapy (PAP) with someone who had approached me to work with him to develop an intensive addiction rehabilitation program that would use psychedelics as a primary focus. I had done extensive research on the topic and was thoroughly convinced that it is, indeed, the wave of the future in terms of trauma and addiction treatment.

So, I agreed to participate in my patient's process, which was orchestrated by a highly experienced facilitator who expertly guided both me and my patient through the entire journey. The intervention had an extraordinary impact and was transformative in that it effectively shut down his addiction and helped him let go of his pain. I was equally impressed with the PAP process itself. It involves three steps: Intentions, Intervention, and Integration. For this discussion about CQ, I will focus only on the first and last parts of the process.

The purpose of the Intention step is to set concrete intentions in the person's mind about what he or she wants to accomplish. Intentions are similar to goals but with an important difference. Goals are usually specific things that you want to accomplish. They are at a micro-level of change that often leads to a change in problematic behavior. An intention can be seen as broader, more macro-level, and more about how you wish to run your life. So, take, for example, an addiction. Let's say the goal would be to stop drinking. But the intention would be much broader, to be more in control of your life, or to be free of the baggage that feeds your addiction.

So, you can see that being intentional about what factors you want to work on can greatly contribute to your change-ability. Intentionality can make the difference between wandering aimlessly through your life and not being purposeful, or working toward a life goal, and being clear about what you want to achieve in your life and what kind of person you want to become. Intentional people have a clear plan about how they wish to run their life.

The last step in PAP is Integration. The way I see it, integration is about bringing your intervention experiences together with the intentions that you established in the first step. Another way of looking at it is that integration allows you to put it all together so that you can implement what you intended to accomplish in the first place.

This is a vital component of CQ because to change yourself you have to take what you are gaining in therapy in the abstract and bring it to a more concrete, actionable level: implementing what you have learned. If you don't actually integrate and then implement what you have experienced in therapy, you haven't really accomplished much in the way of change.

CASE STUDY #6: JEROME

Jerome, a semi-retired criminal attorney, was referred by a colleague who was working with him and his partner, with whom he was having relationship difficulties. He had been married and divorced three times and was struggling with this relationship, as well. He was referred to me because his narcissistic traits were getting in the way of having a successful relationship with his soon-to-be fiancée, and she was having second thoughts about marrying him because of his self-centeredness and inability to be empathetic.

When I asked him what he thought about the fact that he had three failed marriages and that this relationship seemed to be going south as well, he responded, "Well, I guess it's tough to find the right woman." Ugh. I knew at that point that this was not going to be an easy guy to work with. His defenses were sky-high. He then told me that he had been in psychoanalysis for 17 years, three times a week. When I asked him what he had gained from that experience, and what goals he had achieved, he gave me a strange look, as if I were talking to him in Mandarin, and said, "Not a damn thing."

Jerome had not set any intentions before starting his therapy, and as a result, he really had no direction or goal to work toward. For him, it was all about the need to talk about his feelings and his issues de jour, as well as having someone who would be willing to sit and listen to him, without judging or controlling him. In addition, it didn't seem that he had internalized or integrated much of what he did in analysis all those years. According to him, he really hadn't accomplished much of anything concrete or measurable after all of that time, and apparently didn't feel the need for it either. He just wanted to talk and to be heard. As a result, he was still as clueless and self-centered as he had been 17 years ago. The sad truth is that he was right: he hadn't accomplished a thing.

Having a Clear Plan

To build a house, you first have to hire an architect to draw a set of blueprints you can use to plan what you need to do to make sure your house is well-designed, functional, and safe. Without plans, the building process will be chaotic and likely will fail in its goal, resulting in an uninhabitable house.

Similarly, when you embark on a process of change, you also need a clear plan of action that enables you to achieve your therapeutic goals. The development of such a plan is ideally a joint, collaborative effort between you and your therapist. It begins with developing goals and discussing the methods the therapist will employ to help you achieve those goals. In clinical terms, this is a *treatment plan*, and it should be developed and articulated fairly early in the therapeutic process.

The treatment plan usually includes the therapeutic goals you develop with your therapist, the types of interventions or methodologies the therapist will use to help you accomplish those goals, and perhaps a broad outline of the time frame in which you hope to reach these goals. A treatment plan is an important tool, serving as a blueprint to provide the therapeutic direction and structure you need to work toward your goals, track your progress, and evaluate how you're doing in light of your objectives.

Such formal treatment plans are not the only way to establish a plan that can help you accomplish your goals for change. Developing your own more informal plans, perhaps at a more micro level, also can be extremely helpful.

For example, if one of your goals is to gain more control over compulsive eating or overeating, you can develop your own portion control plan, and decide what you will eat at any given meal or make a daily meal plan. Another example would be to plan an exercise regimen if your goal is to lose weight or battle depression. Developing a personalized exercise plan that you can adhere to will invariably make you more likely to achieve your goals in terms of weight, body image, and emotional well-being, as well as change.

Compliance is crucial. Any plan—from a formal treatment plan to a more informal personal plan—won't be worth much unless you can implement it. Compliance with a plan is important for CQ, as discussed in Chapter 10 because real change requires having a plan and sticking to it.

The stronger your ability to follow through with a treatment plan at a formal macro level or a more personal micro level, the higher your CQ will be.

Clueless

Regardless of how sincere or motivated you are about changing, if you don't have a clue about what you specifically need to do in order to change, it's not likely to occur.

People who don't have a clear idea about what they hope to accomplish and, therefore, don't know what they need to do, can wander aimlessly without any idea about what they want to change. To make change more likely, they need a therapist who can help structure, create, and implement a clear action plan for achieving their desired goals. Without that, real change is less likely to occur. The lack of a planned, structured therapeutic strategy can significantly limit one's CQ.

Another level of cluelessness is even more detrimental to one's CQ: While general cluelessness is an obvious detriment, some people have a total lack of awareness that they negatively impact their own lives and the lives of those around them. They are so clueless that they have no idea they need to change. This could relate to a lack of introspection, as discussed in Chapter 12, or to denial stemming from defensiveness, as covered in Chapter 16. This lack of awareness of the need to change is a severe impediment to one's ability to change. Such patients must undergo a painful wake-up call before they can move forward and attempt to change.

People can often be clueless by choice. Many patients I have seen over the years have deliberately decided that they don't want to be clued in about why their marriage is failing or how they affect other people. They prefer to keep their heads in the sand and to live in blissful ignorance of the problems around them. This often includes numbing themselves with whatever addictions or diversions they need to distract them from the painful realities of their dreadful existence. This is different from denial because they realize something is wrong, but they just don't want to deal with it, so they ignore multiple problems and choose to be clueless.

This *modus operandi* can last only so long. Eventually, people who choose to ignore their problems usually end up having to face them when their marriages fall apart, when they lose their job, when their children stop talking to them, and after they lose their last friend—and then, it's often too late. This is very common in situations in which someone has an active addiction and chooses to not work on it. Instead, the addict uses such methods as denial and defensiveness to keep themselves from facing the truth about their self-destructive behaviors. They decide to remain clueless.

If you feel that you may fit this description, then the time has come to stop keeping your "eyes wide shut" and to open them to the harsh realities of your life. Maybe it is finally time to get clued in about how to change things for the better.

Entering this reality may be painful and difficult but choosing to acknowledge your need to change and deciding, at last, to develop a concrete plan about how to achieve your change-related goals may be the best choice you'll ever make.

CASE STUDY #7: REBECCA

As a high-level litigator for a top legal firm, Rebecca was a much sought-after attorney. Many corporations hired her to defend them when they were sued. She was accustomed to being in the courtroom, presenting vigorous arguments to defend her clients, and she was confident in her ability to win cases.

However, she had recently become ill with COVID, which put her out of commission for a while. She had become accustomed to being home, and she liked it, so as she recovered, she began to argue cases via Zoom. When a judge required her to appear in a courtroom for the first time after her illness, she became anxious about being around people. Once in court, she became faint when she began presenting her opening argument. She lost her concentration and had to excuse herself to run to the bathroom to compose herself. However, instead of calming down, she had a full-fledged panic attack in the ladies' room, and instead of returning to the courtroom, she ran to her car and quickly drove home.

In the ensuing months, Rebecca did not leave her house. She relied on Instacart to do her grocery shopping and worked only from home. She never left home, even though all of her firm's other attorneys had returned to the office and were appearing in court when required. When the managing partner called to discuss her inability to appear for work, she broke down and told him that she hadn't been able to leave her house without a panic attack and that she was going to have to resign if he required her to come back to the office.

It appeared that Rebecca not only had a panic disorder, fearing that she would have another panic attack if she went into the courtroom, but she also had developed agoraphobia, an irrational fear of leaving home. Her entire career was in jeopardy, and she was extremely motivated to overcome these fears to save her job and restore her ability to function.

We worked on a comprehensive treatment plan that included medication to control her anxiety, EMDR to desensitize the intense emotions associated with leaving her house and to reprocess what had happened to her, and cognitive-behavioral therapy to dispel the irrational thoughts underlying her fears. It also included systematic desensitization, a behavioral therapy for phobias, that allowed her sequentially to imagine herself leaving her home, going back to work, and eventually returning to the courtroom.

Rebecca was extremely compliant with the treatment regimen and worked hard to regain the confidence she once had in her ability to operate at the highest level, particularly in court. She appreciated the structure of the therapy program, and within a month, she was able to leave her home to go shopping and have lunch with friends. A few weeks later, she returned to the office. We spent several sessions imagining being in the courtroom while doing progressive relaxation exercises, and she participated in a mock trial that allowed her to practice her skills. After all her hard, sincere work, she was reasonably comfortable enough to be able to return to the courtroom and resume her previous level of performance.

CHAPTER 10

FACTOR FIVE:
Integrity vs. Dishonesty

Integrity

The Oxford Dictionary defines integrity as "the quality of being honest and having strong moral principles, moral uprightness." In my mind, especially within the context of CQ, integrity means being forthright and earnest in terms of working toward the goals you set out to accomplish and then doing what you say you will do to meet those goals.

Integrity is a vital component of CQ because it indicates the sincerity of your efforts to change. Many people come up with all kinds of lofty goals, but they really don't have the genuine intention of following through on anything to achieve them. Their goals remain abstract since they make no concrete efforts to do anything about them. They don't have the character, or the integrity, to commit to doing something to make anything actually happen.

Integrity is also important in terms of relationships, in that the people in your life depend on you to come through with what you have committed to do to improve your life, as well theirs. We are not islands, and our behavior affects those around us. When you say that you will commit to therapy, go to a 12-step meeting, or see a psychiatrist to be evaluated for medications, those who love you are relying on you to be honest and to follow through with your commitments. They need to feel that they can rely on you to do what you need to do in order to get the help you need, including following through with treatment recommendations. That is the way to accomplish the goals you've established: becoming healthier and more stable for yourself and for those around you who are affected by your behavior. They need to know that you value your relationships with them enough to take care of the issues that are damaging them and that you are willing to put them above your feelings, discomfort, resistance, and attempts at denial.

Dishonesty

It is equally important not to be dishonest with your therapist. It is not uncommon for people in the therapy process to withhold information (lies of omission) or to be blatantly dishonest about something vital (lies of commission).

However, people who are sincere about change are rigorously honest with their therapist, and they don't withhold information so that the therapist can understand what's really going on and is not in the dark about the true nature of the problem. Therapists will always be better equipped to help you achieve your goals if they have full knowledge of your situation without information gaps or deliberate misinformation, which could be used to hide or distort the truth.

People with integrity go into the process of change with the clear, explicit goal of doing whatever it takes to make the changes that are necessary to live a good, healthy life. They are determined to be straightforward and honest in this endeavor, so they can have the optimal opportunity to succeed in their efforts. It's also just plain smart to give your therapist everything that is needed to help you achieve your goals, rather than handicapping him or her by hiding or obscuring the truth about what's really going on with you. The people I worked with over the years who were rigorously honest with me, and never withheld important feedback about what was going on with them, were the ones who were the most likely to achieve their goals of changing the factors keeping them from being healthy and successful in their relationships.

CASE STUDY #8:
A TALE OF TWO CITIES: ALLAN AND JASON

Recently, I had to deal with two patients who had relapsed in their sex addictions. They had similar situations, except for one thing: integrity.

Allan

A married man in his 30s, Allan suffered emotional and physical abuse from his angry, narcissistic father. He discovered that acting out sexually anesthetizes, albeit temporarily, the pain and anguish from his past (and present). He exhibits symptoms of ADHD and OCD, which manifest in severe impulsivity and compulsive behaviors over which he has been able to show little control. After he acts out, he feels terribly ashamed, and he feels compelled to tell his wife, Joan, because he believes that if he is out of control, then at the very least, he needs to be honest about it. He had come to understand that, if he deceives his wife and she subsequently finds out that he has acted out, it would be a double trauma for her. Not only would she be traumatized because he had violated her trust by acting out, but she would also be even more traumatized by discovering it, instead of his sharing the information with her.

His integrity in being rigorously honest with his wife allowed her to deal with the challenge of his addiction with less anger and more empathy because at least he was honest about it. He tried to be honest with her about everything, and he was earnest about his commitment to treatment. This integrity enabled

Joan to cope with the challenges of his addiction because she had come to trust him and his intentions to truly heal himself.

Jason

In contrast, Jason made it much more difficult for his wife to deal with his sex addiction by lacking integrity. He, too, had a disturbed, abusive father, who left him with insecurity and a lot of emotional pain that Jason learned to neutralize by acting out with pornography and inappropriate online chats. He, too, exhibits symptoms of ADHD and OCD, and he also struggles with impulsive and compulsive behavior.

The difference between Jason and Allan is that Jason had never come clean about his lapses and disturbing behavior, leaving his wife, Julia, to discover his traumatizing activities on her own. This became even more of a betrayal in her eyes, because not only did he not share with her what was going on, he also didn't share it with me—his therapist—either. To her, this represented a significant breach of trust that only compounded the trauma she already had experienced as a result of his actions, thus causing additional strain in an already strained marriage.

Julia's double trauma—finding out that Jason had been betraying her for so long, on top of knowing that he had deceived her previously and was dishonest about his secret life, and that he didn't care enough to share the nature and severity of his problems with her—made things that much more difficult for her to handle.

Joan and Allan were able to work on his addiction and their marriage because she had faith in his ability to approach the healing process with integrity and because he'd been honest with her about his struggles. This brought them closer, and they eventually healed to the point that they had a recommitment ceremony on the first anniversary of his sobriety.

Julia unfortunately experienced numerous further breaches of trust. She was worn down by Jason's inability to be genuine in his recovery or to share with her anything going on inside his private world. She eventually gave up hoping that things would ever change, filed for divorce, and received full custody of their children. Jason eventually lost his job after it was discovered that he was using the company's computer for pornography and illicit chats with random women. He never could muster the integrity to take the process of genuine change seriously.

CHAPTER 11

FACTOR SIX:
Compliant vs. Resistant

Compliant

In simple terms, the definition of compliance is "to obey an order, rule, or request" (Merriam-Webster Dictionary). In our context, compliance means following through with treatment recommendations or suggestions that will assist you in meeting your personal goals. In psychoanalytically oriented therapy sessions, compliance is less of an issue, because typically there are no homework assignments, recommendations, or things patients need to do before their next session. There may be strategic, carefully worded suggestions, but rarely do they come with the explicit expectation that compliance is necessary. However, in cognitive-behavioral therapy, specific treatment goals are clearly delineated, and assignments and recommendations are explicitly stated as something the patient is expected to accomplish, usually by the next session. Therefore, compliance is essential if these goals are to be accomplished.

If you hope to achieve the changes you need to make to function at the level you are striving for by coming to therapy or working on yourself in general, there are concrete things you need to do or need to do differently, in order for those changes to occur. The general rule is that the more effort you put into the process, the more likely change is to happen. Or in other words, borrowing from 12-step programs, "the more you work it, the more it works."

So, what does compliance look like in real terms? Well, we can start with making sure that you show up at your appointments, and on time. That is a basic, but essential, element of compliance, without which you are less likely to achieve your recovery or treatment goals. It also shows, as discussed in the previous chapter, how motivated you really are to change. Compliance also involves following through promptly on specific homework assignments. Many of my patients either "forget" their homework, choose to ignore it, or partially complete it, making insufficient genuine effort to accomplish the task.

Being compliant can make a real difference in carving significant inroads into managing your problems and progressing toward your stated goals. On the other hand, noncompliance can actually make the therapy process, or whatever you are doing to work on yourself, a waste of time. Passively attending sessions or promising to do things for your partner that would represent change and not following through will impede your ability to achieve the changes you must accomplish to reach your overarching goals, such as saving your marriage or your job, or reconnecting with your children. It can also provoke resentment and alienation from the people you're trying to reconnect with in the first place. The bottom line is that if you aren't willing to follow through on what you've committed to do, nothing is likely to change.

Resistance

Noncompliance usually reflects some sort of resistance, a limiting factor that diminishes CQ. Resistance can take many forms and can result from a variety of factors.

As previously mentioned, resistance can come from passive-aggression, in which the patient does not express resistance directly, but shows it indirectly through noncompliance. Passive-aggressive individuals often don't have the core to be assertive and express their feelings explicitly but, rather, they show their displeasure in passive ways that indirectly reflect their negative feelings. It's often important to confront this directly, but sensitively, to allow space for the person to express these feelings in a more straightforward manner, so that open communication can ensue. Often, dealing with noncompliance directly through clear, respectful discussions can help people work through their issues, so the patient can shift gears and become more compliant in following through on expected, necessary activities.

Individuals with narcissistic traits can be resistant because they are typically sensitive about giving up control or having discussions that focus on their flaws. They are often deeply resentful of, if not downright hostile about being in the patient role because they can be delusional about where their problem lies. They have developed distorted narratives to convince themselves that the problem is with all the other people in their lives and that those people's flaws and reactions are the real cause of whatever problems exist.

Since people with narcissistic tendencies are also usually quite sensitive about being controlled and are more comfortable being in the position of being in control, they often can be non-compliant in meeting their commitments. Since they are also convinced that they are not the problem, they believe they shouldn't have to do the work that's necessary to fix the problem. They also resist being compliant because they misconstrue suggestions and assignments as attempts to control them, instead of seeing these activities as ways to facilitate making therapeutic progress toward their own goals.

Depressed people also often have difficulty following through on steps that are necessary to bring about change because they lack the emotional and physical energy to follow through on almost everything they face. They are too drained and depleted to exert any sustained effort. Just getting through the day requires tremendous energy, so doing more is beyond them, even when the measures they are supposed to carry out would otherwise seem basic and readily achieved. They might not be actively resistant to doing the required work, but they resist because they simply can't conjure up the requisite effort.

People with obsessive-compulsive traits also may resist complying with what is expected of them therapeutically, for a variety of reasons. Quite typically, they find it difficult to follow through on a lot of expectations because of their severe perfectionism. This causes them to avoid or procrastinate on tasks that seem overwhelming to them because they fear that they may not do them quite perfectly or because of the amount of anxiety the expectation of perfection causes. But, people with OCD can also be very compliant, almost to a compulsive degree, so we can't generalize the problem of non-compliance to all individuals with OCD traits. Nevertheless, the unrealistic self-expectations that these patients often put on themselves can cause emotional paralysis that results in them not following through on activities that are necessary for them to carry out in order to make progress.

So, what can be done about such resistance? Once again, honest self-reflection about why change is needed and what is needed for change to happen can help overcome resistance. Allowing your therapist or significant other to have a frank discussion with you about the possible reasons for your resistance—and to explore ways to overcome it—could be instrumental in achieving some sort of breakthrough. This could hopefully facilitate your transition out of a non-compliant pattern and toward more of a partnership that can help get things back on track toward real progress.

Once again, contingency management can be a tool for righting the ship. If change is required to maintain a marriage, stay in the home, or keep a job, then noncompliance with treatment recommendations can invoke a threat of negative consequences if things don't change in the right direction. Unfortunately, I have had to remind too many patients about the potential consequences of a lack of compliance with their commitments to get them back on track. It often can feel rather adolescent to have to break the process down to incurring consequences, but that often comes with the territory.

Finally, a noncompliant patient might need to take a break from therapy or leave the marital home temporarily, given his or her obvious resistance. If you are a non-compliant patient, this could give you an opportunity to reflect on why you are in therapy in the first place and to consider the potential ramifications of failure to progress toward your stated goals. I have had to suspend therapy on occasion because of non-compliance, and though it did result in ultimate termination at times, in many cases it forced the person to be more introspective about his or her resistance, to come back with a renewed effort to comply, and to be more generally cooperative with the process.

CASE STUDY #9: LEVI

Levi, 35, is a wildly creative serial entrepreneur. He successfully builds out-of-the-box companies and sells them for a huge profit. He then creates his next venture, which turns out to be even more successful.

I frequently see his creativity and energy level in individuals who have been diagnosed with ADHD, because their brains are often wired in such a way that they can envision things no one else can think of, and they see things in a different light.

However, his impulsivity, irresponsibility with regard to his family, and his lack of follow-through made it difficult, if not impossible, for him to maintain a stable relationship. His wife, Carrie, came in for treatment because she could no longer tolerate his behaviors. She told him he had to come to therapy if he wanted her to stay in the marriage.

Specifically, his inability to be even remotely on time for virtually anything, his impulsive rages, and his resistance to helping her with their young children had alienated her to the point that she was contemplating divorce. Additionally, he smoked marijuana nightly, and he also abused alcohol on too many occasions. None of this conformed to her need for order, predictability, and stability.

From the outset, Levi proclaimed that he didn't want to lose Carrie or his family and that he, at least in theory, was willing to work on changing. However, his refusal to even consider medication because he didn't like the way it made him feel (that is, controlled and "not himself"), made treatment quite challenging.

He also either came quite late to each session or missed his appointments entirely and gave some dubious reason. This made any real progress virtually impossible. He ignored homework assignments or minimally pursued them. At some point, we both concluded that therapy was not working for either of us. We terminated therapy, and shortly thereafter, Carrie filed for divorce.

A few months later, I heard again from Levi, who apparently hadn't believed that Carrie would actually take action to divorce him. He asked me if I would be willing to try working with him again. I told him that I would, but that my agreement was contingent on him having an evaluation by a psychiatrist, taking whatever medication the doctor prescribed, going to 12-step meetings for his drug and alcohol abuse, and taking the commitment to therapy and follow-up assignments more seriously. He agreed, and after being diagnosed and given the right medication, he returned to my office.

He reported that, as a result of the medication, which required him to stop using marijuana and alcohol, he was able to see how destructive his previous behaviors had been to himself and his marriage. He was pleased with his ability to be more responsible and in control of himself. Once he became more compliant with the requirements of therapy, he started to show real change in his partnership with Carrie.

He took her needs for stability and support more seriously. The relationship became a win-win, in that she felt that she, finally, had the partner she needed. He also felt much better about himself because he could be more like the father and husband he wanted to be but hadn't been able to be previously because of ADHD and substance abuse. She eventually withdrew the petition for divorce. More recently, she reported to me that their marriage and her life in general had "never been better."

CHAPTER 12

FACTOR SEVEN:
Stable vs. Unstable

Stable

What does it mean to be stable, and how does that relate to the concept of CQ? Well, stability can mean a wide range of things. It can mean consistency or the ability to be consistent over time. Or, it can mean being emotionally or behaviorally healthy and having the ability to be consistently appropriate and effective in living your life.

Stability may also relate to your reliability and ability to follow through on your commitments, an essential ingredient of CQ. You can't realistically accomplish much in the way of real change if you are unable or unwilling to do what is necessary to complete the tasks and assignments that you accept. Being stable also means coming to your therapy appointments regularly and on time so that you can consistently carry out the work that is necessary for change.

Stability also involves the ability to be emotionally stable. People who are emotionally regulated and in control of their feelings are far more likely to be successful in their attempts to change than are people who are emotionally dysregulated.

Stable people are also more likely to have the emotional resources to focus on what they need to change and the wherewithal to make those changes. They aren't distracted or depleted by grappling with inner turmoil on a sometimes-daily basis, so they have more energy and a higher ability to deal with the challenges of the change process.

Finally, being stable means others can trust you to take your responsibilities seriously and to prioritize the changes you are asked to make. Many patients have come to me ramped up to do the work of changing, very excited and enthusiastic about therapy, and then, after a relatively short period of time, they lose interest or become distracted and drift out of therapy. Other priorities take over, and they lose the drive to do the work required to achieve a successful outcome.

All of these elements of stability are vital for a high CQ.

Let's look at the types of mental disorders that interfere with one's ability to be stable since they can make change difficult if not impossible.

Unstable: Mental Disorders

Within the context of this discussion about CQ, stability can mean the absence of a major mental illness that would preclude a person from being able to function effectively. People with major mental illnesses such as schizophrenia or bipolar disorder, in particular, are inherently unstable. They suffer from debilitating hallucinations, delusions, dramatic mood instability, and other manifestations of psychosis. All of these challenges make it all but impossible to be stable enough to achieve any measure of meaningful change. In such cases, the therapeutic goal is usually just to achieve some degree of stability, rather than any actual therapeutic change.

People with Borderline Personality Disorder (BDP) are often inherently unstable in their thoughts, actions, perceptions, ego states, and identities. Their overall sense of being is so fluid that the only thing stable in their lives is their instability. They can flip their attitude toward people or the therapy process on a dime, leaving therapists and family members to wonder what happened to the person who was so motivated and determined to change. People with this disorder can often have very unstable feelings toward other people in general or toward their therapist in particular, often varying between overidealizing and devaluing the people in their lives, including the professionals who are trying to help them.

Working therapeutically with borderline people can be quite challenging, to say the least, and living with them can be downright maddening. Dealing with emotional intensity and dysregulation can be a daunting task, but with the right help, people with BPD can indeed change, although their individual degree of instability can influence BPD's effect on CQ. Therapeutic programs, such as Dialectic Behavioral Therapy (DBT), can be extremely effective in teaching people with this disorder the skills they need to achieve greater stability in their lives and to work toward the therapeutic goals they have established for themselves. Externally imposed goals are generally less effective.

DBT includes four modules that can be critically helpful in a patient's progress toward attaining a greater degree of stability: Distress Tolerance, Mindfulness, Emotional Regulation, and Relationship Skills, all of which can be valuable in increasing CQ.

Other disorders also can have a significant effect on one's stability. Cyclothymia, a milder form of bipolar disorder, is often quite similar to the disorder referred to as Bipolar II. It is characterized by bouts of hypomania—a subclinical, less dramatic type of mania—alternating with periods of mild depression. Although people with this type of disorder rarely become psychotic, they struggle with emotional and behavioral stability because of their inability to regulate their moods. They can either be too high to be stable participants in therapy or too low to have the energy to do much of anything to work on changing themselves. This obviously has an adverse effect on CQ, unless the person's symptoms can be stabilized in therapy and with medication.

As mentioned before, people with clinical depression also can find it difficult to work on changing themselves because they lack the drive or motivation to do the work necessary for change. They also struggle with stability, because their bouts of depression interfere with their ability to lead stable lives. Often, their only goal is to stay stable so they can function at some acceptable level. Going beyond that to achieve sustainable change is often quite difficult, if not out of reach.

Finally, people who have experienced severe trauma and have symptoms of PTSD can also demonstrate marked emotional and behavioral instability. Flashbacks, startle responses, and emotional reactivity, as well as vulnerability to being highly triggered by situations associated with past traumas, can all contribute to significant instability. Treatment strategies that can be instrumental in stabilizing a traumatized person include Eye Movement Desensitization and Reprocessing (EMDR), which can be extremely effective in healing past traumas, and Internal Family Systems Therapy (IFS), which strives to identify and heal the fragmented parts of the personality that evolved from trauma,

So, what can you do to become more stable, gain the ability to improve your CQ, and work on your capacity to change? In my experience, the combination of intensive cognitive-behavioral therapy and mood-stabilizing medication, plus DBT, IFS, and EMDR for any trauma underlying the instability, can be most effective in helping someone become more stable. Perhaps most important is the patient's macro-level awareness of the need to be more stable in thought, emotion, and behavior. Patients at that level must also make a commitment to do what they say they will in order to accomplish the necessary work. If you are beset by a severe mental illness, this may be the best formula for becoming more stable in your daily life and achieving the goal of maximum changeability.

CASE STUDY #10: LINCOLN

As a bright, creative millennial, Lincoln had tremendous potential in his position as a marketing analyst for a social media platform. However, a history of erratic performance and emotional outbursts landed him in my office, undertaking therapy as a requirement from his company's HR department. The company sent him for treatment because of his work patterns. Lincoln would work tirelessly and put in long hours for weeks, and then crash and not show up for work for several days, without contacting his supervisor. His colleagues had experienced several incidents in which he had lost control of his emotions, at times getting angry and aggressive, and at other times having intense episodes of remorseful crying when his boss or HR called him out for his behavior.

It appeared that Lincoln had built up a history of emotional intensity and instability throughout his adolescent years, despite having many academic achievements and extracurricular accomplishments. Concerned about his emotional issues, his parents had sent him to a counselor who focused only on the relationship problems he wanted to talk about and did not address his obvious underlying issues.

Therapy with Lincoln was challenging. He started enthusiastically and was "all in," almost to an exaggerated degree. That lasted for a few weeks, and then he began to skip our appointments, sometimes with flimsy excuses, and other times not even bothering to let me know that he wasn't going to come in.

I had no choice but to let his HR officer know that Lincoln was not complying with the therapeutic contract he had signed. When he returned to therapy, he was enraged and abusive to me. He was very angry I had told his company that he was blowing off his commitment to attend therapy sessions regularly.

It became apparent that Lincoln had an undiagnosed case of bipolar disorder, and when I finally was able to get him to be calm enough to discuss the real issue underlying his ongoing problems, he seemed to be open to working on it. He made an appointment with a psychiatrist, who prescribed a mood stabilizer for his unstable emotions and mood swings. Unfortunately, he didn't like the way the medication numbed his feelings, and he abruptly stopped taking it. He continued to be unstable and emotionally reactive, and therefore he was unable to make any progress in therapy because of his inconsistency, as well as the other effects of bipolar disorder. His company eventually fired him, and he landed in a psychiatric facility after a suicide attempt.

When last I heard from him, he was working at home as a freelance computer programmer and was completely uninterested in continuing therapy. He said he "was fine" and didn't need to work on himself anymore, even though he had lost two other jobs in the interim for the same behavior that cost him his first job.

CHAPTER 13

FACTOR EIGHT:
Introspective vs. Blocked

Introspective

Quite often, a successful change process requires the ability to look inside yourself and to take an objective view of your behavior, your motivations, and the impact you are having on the people around you. This also can involve your ability to ask yourself tough questions such as, "What am I doing to alienate the people I am supposed to love?" or "How do I really want to show up in my life?" Other questions could include, "What do I need to change to be fully functional?" or "What should my goals be to become the best that I can be?"

These are all aspects of the concept of introspection, which can be defined as: "The examination or observation of one's own mental and emotional processes" (Merriam-Webster Dictionary). Introspection is a significant prerequisite for change, an important ingredient in the CQ formula. We can't expect to change if we lack insight into why we need to change in the first place. The ability to be introspective allows us to do some honest soul-searching and objectively evaluate how we are doing relative to how we wish to be doing.

There is a rather old psychological metric called "the actual versus the ideal self-differential." Roughly speaking, this measures the difference between how we see or feel about ourselves versus how we wish we could or should be. As the theory goes, the greater the differential between our actual and our ideal self, the lower our self-esteem, the higher our risk for depression, and the more likely we are to be experiencing general problems in the way we live. Conversely, the smaller the differential, the more emotionally healthy we are, and the more life satisfaction we are likely to experience.

However, there is a different way of viewing this dynamic. The more introspective we are in looking at this differential between the actual self versus the ideal self, the more motivated we can be to do the work toward becoming closer to our ideal self. Introspection allows us the ability to realize that we are not functioning in ways that we would ideally like to function. This can be a powerful motivator to get us to want to change and, ultimately, to do the work that is required for us to accomplish the changes we want.

Introspection can also be a reality check that can give us an accurate sense of how we are doing in our lives, what we are proud of and feel good about, what we aren't so happy about, and what needs to change as a result. These reality checks can help keep us grounded in reality and prevent us from giving in to self-distortions that convince us, "We are good; it's everyone else that's the problem." Being reality-oriented and honest with ourselves can be a significant motivator for change and that's why it's also so important to your CQ.

Blocked

People who lack the ability to be introspective, to look inside themselves, are typically emotionally blocked, which can happen for a variety of reasons. Most likely, they are blocked because their psychological defenses keep them from taking a good, honest look at themselves, most often because they lack the ego strength to face the truth about themselves. These defenses allow them to convince themselves that they do not need to be introspective, because, as mentioned above, they are not the problem. Narcissistic people often fall into this category because they must project blame onto others since they are too emotionally fragile to face the true reality about themselves and their culpability.

People who are traumatized and emotionally overwhelmed can also be blocked in their ability to be introspective. They simply lack the psychological wherewithal to be able to make the effort. When a person is hanging by a thread emotionally and can barely muster the strength to get through the day, it's unreasonable to expect that he or she is going to have the resources to even start to think about improving themselves or working on the things they need to change.

The same applies to people who are clinically depressed. They also lack the emotional fortitude needed to start looking inside themselves and evaluating what needs to change. They either can't bring themselves to be introspective because they are too shut down, or they can't stop focusing on everything that is wrong with them. This is really a form of self-devaluing, rather than healthy introspection. Either way, they can't bring themselves to be introspective in a way that can lead to meaningful change.

Anxious or obsessive people are also blocked in their ability to be introspective. They are too caught up in just trying to function or in trying to cope with whatever is triggering them to bring themselves to stop and reflect about, "What is going on here, and what do I need to do to get myself under control?" Their ability to be introspective is not inherently impaired, but their emotions overwhelm them, limiting their capacity to take the time or make the effort to even think about anything other than how paralyzing their anxiety is from moment to moment.

Some people lack the capacity to introspect at all. They are intrinsically blocked in their ability to process their emotions. Alexithymia is a condition in which people can't identify or describe their feelings. These people often can't cognitively look inside themselves or objectively see themselves or the issues they are facing. This fairly unknown cognitive/emotional disability affects more people than we realize, and it can severely limit their ability to be in touch generally with what's inside of them.

So, what can be done to help yourself or other people who are blocked in their ability to be introspective? Of course, it depends on the reason for the blockage. People who are narcissistic and defensive about their shortcomings need a balance between empathy and support on the one hand and reality and accountability on the other. A therapist must engage them in a trustworthy, respectful manner and, at the same time, gently begin the process of asking questions that can open them up, ever so slowly, to take an honest look at themselves, so they can start to come around and see what they haven't been able to face about themselves.

Using the Socratic method therapeutically can be very effective in accomplishing this goal. Instead of beating someone over the head to get them to face the truth about themselves, I ask carefully selected questions to try to help them come to realizations about their flaws on their own, without their defenses getting in the way. I often use the Socratic method with defensive patients because I know that confronting them directly will usually backfire and result in them shutting down emotionally or shutting me out. You can use this method on yourself by asking yourself pertinent questions about the reality of your situation, such as, "What am I doing to bring out all this hostility in my co-workers?" or "What does it say about me that I am about to get divorced for a third time?" These questions force you to turn inward and to reflect on your contribution to the problems that you are facing, instead of reflexively focusing on what's wrong with everyone else.

People who are anxious or depressed have to work on these issues first—and get to a better place of emotional equilibrium—before they can begin to be introspective and process things thoroughly. Trying to do soul-searching when you are in these unstable states of being can be futile and often counterproductive. Treating the anxiety and depression first can then open you up to begin the process of introspection so that you can take a good look inside and start to think about how and why you get so anxious and depressed in the first place, as well as what you can do about it.

People who have processing issues and difficulty with the cognitive ability to be introspective can benefit from cognitive therapy that can identify, step-by-step, how to think about what may be going on that is causing them so many problems. This is a matter of training your mind to look inside yourself and search for possible reasons for your problems or learning what it is about yourself that might be contributing to these issues.

The bottom line is that many of us find it difficult to self-reflect honestly and to be introspective about ourselves and what may be wrong with the ways we process (or don't process) our experiences or react to triggers. If you relate to any of this discussion, it may be helpful to realize first that you are emotionally blocked and to explore ways with your therapist, or a trusted loved one, to unblock yourself and become more open to exploring things about yourself that you have found difficult or threatening to examine. You may find that it is more gratifying to know what the problems are and to explore how to remedy them than it is to stay clueless and in denial. Remember: With knowledge comes power, and you need both to really change yourself.

CASE STUDY #11: BRUCE

Having worked as a mid-level manager in a high-tech company for several years, Bruce was a consultant for the company when he came to see me. He was frustrated that he didn't seem to be able to move up the corporate ladder and develop his career as he had envisioned. He was still mid-level and although he had applied for several positions, he had been passed up for each one. That left him wondering what was keeping him from moving ahead in his career. He was contemplating finding a job in another company, but his fear of change was holding him back from taking the first step to make that happen.

It was clear from the outset that Bruce clearly lacked insight into the reasons he was having difficulty in his present employment. When I asked what kind of feedback he could recall from past performance reviews, he claimed that he couldn't remember any specifics and that he didn't have a clue why he kept being passed up for all those promotions. I asked him if he would give me consent to speak to his supervisor, John, for some feedback, and he agreed. The information John gave me clarified things significantly. He told me that although Bruce was hard-working and basically competent, his co-workers and those he supervised found him difficult to connect to and quite shallow.

His emotional depth in interactions was clearly limited, and others found him robotic and transactional, as opposed to being relatable. They respected his work ethic and ability to get things done, but at a human level, his ability to understand people and develop relationships was quite limited.

It became clear that Bruce's inability to be introspective and to understand his interpersonal impact was the underlying reason for his lack of career advancement. He apparently had no capacity for real insight, and his ability to understand the complexities of how to develop a relationship and how to interact in a meaningful way suffered as a result. It became apparent that he was probably on the Autism spectrum and could have been diagnosed with the now unused diagnosis of Asperger's Syndrome Disorder, a pervasive developmental disorder characterized by a lack of social awareness; an inability to feel or show empathy; narrow, idiosyncratic interests; odd behaviors and speech patterns; and perhaps most important, a lack of insight and an inability to be introspective. This latter deficit made any real therapeutic progress difficult, although, through behavior therapy and empathy training, Bruce was able to learn specific interpersonal behaviors that made him somewhat more effective as a supervisor. However, when we last spoke, he was still waiting for that promotion.

CHAPTER 14

FACTOR NINE:
Analytical vs. Concrete

Analytical

Analytical people tend to want to understand things at a deeper level and have the necessary intellectual capacity to do so. They don't take things at face value, but rather they tend to go beyond a superficial understanding of how things happen in their lives, or about themselves, and to try to comprehend the inherent complexities.

To be analytical is to be "able to identify and define problems, extract key information from data, and develop workable solutions for the problems identified in order to test and verify the cause of the problem and develop solutions to resolve the problems identified" (Chicago State University). More simply, analytical people are good at identifying problems and finding solutions for them. This characteristic obviously correlates to high CQ because analytical people are more oriented toward problem-solving and are therefore more likely to work on themselves and the problems they face.

Analytical people are thinkers whose minds are not content

with the simple meaning of a concept or an idea. They analyze what they hear or read to reach a better understanding of the complexities of situations or relationships and to improve their ability to handle them in the future. They tend to keep thinking about something when others are ready to move on. They aren't satisfied with a simple comment or explanation but rather want to keep processing the information to gain a deeper understanding.

Is there a perfect correlation between analytical ability and changeability? I think likely not. Just because you are an analytical person doesn't mean that you will use that ability constructively to achieve the higher purpose of meaningful, personal change. Some people who use their superior intellectual abilities to argue, obfuscate, and otherwise obstruct dialogues that can lead to change end up sabotaging efforts to get them to change. They can manipulate such efforts by using their analytical abilities to deflect the discussion away from the reality that they need to change, or to argue that they aren't the ones who need to change.

It is also possible that people can overthink and be too analytical, as in the case of people with OCD. These people get stuck in the hamster wheel of anxious obsessiveness that leads them only to further anxiety. The difference between obsessive thinking and being appropriately analytical is that analyzing something is a means of processing information or a step toward a definitive end, and when you have reached a conclusion, the analyzing is over and you can move on to something else. However, people who are obsessive keep analyzing, over and over again without stopping, and never reach a logical conclusion. Their thinking becomes out of control and anxiety overtakes them in the end. It's vitally important to make sure that you're being analytical and processing instead of being endlessly obsessive if you want to contribute positively to a higher CQ and an enhanced ability to change.

Narcissists, who are often intelligent and manipulative, frequently fit this description of outmaneuvering family and friends who wish for them to change by arguing against the points their loved ones make and deflecting blame onto others. They can be highly effective in using their analytical abilities to dodge the responsibility to change. So, if you are smart and have the capacity to be analytical, be smart enough to not use those talents against your ability to grow and develop. Instead, use your gifts to work on being the person you want to be.

Concrete

As opposed to being analytical, concrete individuals have a limited ability to understand their lives at a deeper level. They tend to be satisfied with attaining a basic, simpler understanding of events, and they lack the capacity, or the will, to delve deeper into the complexities of their lives. They aren't interested in discussing the issues that affect them because they feel overwhelmed by their complexity and prefer to ignore or compartmentalize their problems. Change is often threatening to them because it requires sustained efforts to analyze and more deeply understand why they are having difficulties and what they can do about it. This level of introspection may be beyond their capacity.

Concrete people often live their lives from day to day. They tend to want to just "go with the flow," instead of having any ambition about making any meaningful changes in their lives. Concrete people are complacent and wish to keep things simple, rather than complicate their lives with challenging and complex discussions involving their need to change. They deal with efforts to get them to confront their flaws and weaknesses with resistance. They often claim that those who are making these demands are just trying to make things difficult and unnecessarily complicated. They just want to KISS (Keep It Simple Stupid) and not be bothered with obtuse discussions about relationships or communication problems. It's just too much for them. They prefer to have only transactional interactions, talking about things that need to be done or random people or events, rather than reflecting on their relationships or their need to change.

Becoming more analytical can be challenging for some people. First, this ability is often seen as something that we are born with, and not something we can modify. Analytical ability can indeed be highly inheritable, but that doesn't mean that you can't succeed at being less concrete and more analytical. Instead of avoiding discussions that your partner or other significant others feel are necessary to deal with seemingly complex issues, try to force yourself to engage. Instead of avoiding these interactions, allow yourself to try to understand what they are communicating to you at a deeper level. You may find that your ability to comprehend deeper motives and feelings is greater than you realize—and so is the reward.

CASE STUDY #12: RENEE

As a child of Holocaust survivors, Renee experienced a tremendous amount of what Internal Family Systems calls, "legacy burdens." Her earliest childhood memories were horrifying stories of her parents' experiences in various concentration camps and ghettos where they were brutalized by Nazi guards. Endless stories of faceless relatives who were invariably murdered by different methods were overwhelming for a developing child, like Renee. She was the oldest of four daughters, all of whom developed various mental health issues. She was also deeply affected by her father Reinhard's periodic reactions to traumatizing nightmares. He would awake, screaming in the middle of the night, turn the lights on, grab his daughters, and run outside to escape from the Nazis, who were, in his mind, chasing after him.

Renee decided to enter treatment because she was having trouble regulating her intense emotions, and she was unable to remain stable for her husband and children. For the first time, her husband, Jake, gave her an ultimatum that if she didn't get help, he would have to separate from her and take their two kids, because he could no longer stand by and see them being affected by her erratic, intense reactions toward them. They were beginning to show signs of significant anxiety, and their academic performance had deteriorated so much that the school's counselor had reached out to him because of the school's concern about their well-being.

During our first session, it was clear that Renee was incredibly bright. Her ability to understand and analyze complex concepts was quite impressive, but it was equally apparent that she also could misuse her obvious superior intellectual abilities to construct intricate defenses to defend or explain away her behaviors, or to find ways to project blame onto her husband, the children, the weather, her hormones—anything but her own actions.

When I attempted to challenge her and shine some light on how she was sabotaging treatment through her machinations to avoid responsibility, she became enraged and eventually stormed out of my office. She texted me that she needed to "take a break" from therapy, and I didn't hear back from her for several months.

When I heard back from her months later, she told me that Jake had moved out and filed for a legal separation, and that he was determined to take the children with him. She was clearly desperate and acknowledged that she "blew it" with our therapy. She wanted to start over and said she was committed to doing whatever it took to get her family back together.

Over time, she was able to see that she was exhibiting symptoms of borderline personality disorder (BPD), as manifested by emotional intensity and dysregulation, rageful reactions, black-and-white judgments, and alternating between devaluing her husband and children, and then overly ingratiating herself with them. This diagnosis gave her a conceptual framework for understanding her instability and its impact on her family. She made a conscious choice to use her analytical abilities to reach a deeper understanding of how the traumas of her childhood had contributed to the development of her personality and the destructive behaviors that resulted.

As soon as she committed to being "all in" and to researching trauma and BPD, Renee was able to develop a deeper understanding of how BPD develops and manifests itself. She also learned how to apply skills from Dialectical Behavioral Therapy (DBT) training to self-regulate and work on becoming a more stable and mindful mother and wife.

Within several months, through intense one-on-one therapy, as well as marital and family therapy, the family was reunited. Its dynamics changed so much that Renee and Jake became closer and more loving toward each other, and the emotional issues that the children were exhibiting diminished significantly. Once Renee made the conscious choice to use her cognitive abilities to help her heal, instead of to sabotage her treatment, her motivation and ability to change increased dramatically. This led to a more organic transformative change.

CHAPTER 15

FACTOR TEN:
Flexibility vs. Rigidity

Flexibility

It seems obvious that if you want to change, the ability to be flexible is an important factor. Why? Well, let's look at what the word "flexible" actually means. The Oxford English dictionary defines flexibility as being, "ready and able to change so as to adapt to different conditions or situations."

This seems to indicate that a flexible person can "go with the flow," adapt to changing circumstances, and do what is necessary to adjust as the need arises. For instance, responding to the needs of significant others who have come to find it difficult to interact or function with you is an example of an evolving circumstance that requires you to change yourself in some way in response. The situation has become pressing enough to require you to work on how you deal with those you love.

Flexible people can respond to such a challenge by understanding the problem, considering various options, and making the efforts needed to respond to the challenge. Such challenges do not threaten them. Instead, they can embrace the opportunity to work on themselves to improve their relationships.

Flexible people also tend to be easy-going, relaxed, and open-minded. They look at problems as opportunities for growth and personal development, as opposed to disturbances to avoid or disdain. Their mindset is generally malleable, in that they don't feel the need to hold on rigidly to their beliefs about what is right and wrong. They can entertain the possibility that things are more complex and less absolute. People who are flexible also don't feel the need to cling to their ideas or argue their points. Instead, they allow others to express their opinions, feelings, or needs without pushing back if they don't agree.

Flexibility can also manifest itself through the ability to be adventurous. People who like adventure tend to be spontaneous and not rigorously programmed, attributes often associated with flexibility. Adventurous people like to experience things as they come, and they enjoy surprises. They don't require life to be predictable, but rather they can embrace the unpredictable.

Personal flexibility is often associated with life satisfaction, achievement, and greater adjustment to circumstances, in general. It is often a predictor of someone's overall effectiveness and success in relationships. That makes sense because being in a relationship requires having quite a bit of flexibility so you can respond to another person's needs and feelings.

Generally, then, we expect flexible people to be more open to change and, in fact, more capable of change, thus resulting in a higher CQ than that of those who are more rigid, a topic which we now will examine in greater detail.

Rigidity

Rigid people, as a general rule, are resistant to change because they want or need things to stay the same. Change threatens them because it represents a departure from what is known, comfortable, and predictable. Rigid people would rather remain the same, even if the status quo causes them and others to suffer. At least, it is a known state, as opposed to the unknown state that is represented by change. Inflexible people are often stuck because of their rigidity; they find themselves unable to move forward with any effort to change because the threat that change represents far outweighs any perceived benefit they think they could derive from the effort it would take to change.

Different clinical profiles are often associated with rigidity. Perhaps the most prominent of these is Obsessive-Compulsive Personality Disorder (OCDP), which personifies the concept of rigidity. People with OCPD are, by nature, typically very rigid and resistant to any efforts to get them to change. Their perfectionism makes it very difficult for them to even be aware that they need to change, much less to be able to do whatever is necessary to make an actual change. They stubbornly resist other people's attempts to get them to see how they affect those near them, and they refuse to acknowledge how alienating their behaviors are. Their rigidity also leads to issues of control, involving their attempts to control others. They perceive any attempts to get them to change as being efforts to control them. These people tend to find it very difficult to change and helping them become more changeable often requires a lot of therapeutic effort.

People with actual obsessive-compulsive disorder (OCD), which is a bona fide anxiety disorder characterized by severe obsessive thinking and/or compulsive behaviors, can also be rigid in their thought patterns and behaviors. The anxiety usually associated with OCD often prevents those who suffer from it from being flexible because the prospect of changing or diverting from their strict internal script of how things should be keeps them from allowing any real change. Their obsessive thinking can literally hijack their minds, causing them to be cognitively stuck and incapable of moving forward in their behavior or in their lives.

Narcissistic people are often rigidly convinced that they aren't the problem in relationships, but that those around them are the *real* problems. They are also stuck, but within their own rigid narrative of what is real, as opposed to what is objectively true. These distortions of reality can attain levels of delusional proportions. The rigid thinking of narcissistic people often manifests in the defensive mechanisms they employ to protect their fragile egos. Narcissists have diffi- culty changing because facing the reality that they need to change is entirely too threatening for them, as is confronting the truth about themselves. Their defensive personality struc- ture prevents them from being able to be honest enough with themselves to even accept the reality that they are the ones who need to change—and not those around them.

People on the autism spectrum also find it difficult to change. I'm not necessarily referring here to autism itself, but to those who previously would have been referred to or diagnosed as having Asperger's Disorder. They are often very rigid in their thinking and behavior. This disorder is neurologically very much related to OCD, and there are a lot of overlapping symptoms. This means that they have traits in common, one of which is cognitive and behavioral rigidity. Stereotypical behaviors—the unusual, repetitive behaviors often seen in individuals on the autism spectrum—are also manifestations of behavioral rigidity that are often difficult, if not impossible, to contain.

So, what does this all mean for you? Are you more of a flexible kind of person, one who goes with the flow and can modify yourself when needed? Or, are you a more rigid person who finds it difficult to change, even when change is necessary? If you find that you fit more of the latter description, then it may be important for you to find ways to work on being more flexible and more open to change. Be bold and look for ways to change your routine; try to be more deliberate in looking at things from a different angle, instead of seeing things only one way—usually your way.

Also, try to be more open to hearing feedback about yourself from those who love and care about you. Don't shut them down or argue. This exercise is also a way of becoming more flexible in the way you see yourself, without using defense mechanisms to deflect away painful truths about yourself. Flexibility is a crucial component of CQ, and it is something you can work on in very concrete and creative ways that can help you become an agent of change—for yourself.

CASE STUDY #13: LORETTA

Loretta is a CPA with two teenagers, Luke and Larry, who required her to maintain a great deal of order and predictability in her life. She grew up in a family that was chaotic due to her father's severe alcoholism and her mother's unstable personality, which led to random outbursts and irrational emotional reactions to relatively minor infractions. She was highly critical of Loretta and often blamed her, even when she was a child, for triggering her father's drinking.

As a result, Loretta developed strong perfectionistic personality traits and became very rigid in her expectations of her family. She had strict rules for her household and left no possibility of including her family's input or of having any flexibility in the rules. Her harsh treatment of the boys, and her inability to be flexible, resulted in their anger and oppositional-defiant behavior—reactions that only made her rigidity that much more severe.

In both boys, this cycle resulted in a tremendous amount of rebellious behavior and resentment. This especially affected Luke, the older one, because he was a senior in high school and felt that he needed more autonomy in making decisions so he could live his life the way he wished. Even just months away from leaving for college, he still had to submit to the same 10:30 pm curfew that Loretta instituted when he was 13, even though his friends could all be out until at least 1 am. Loretta also would not even discuss the possibility of Luke driving the family car, although he had earned his license, because she felt that it was too dangerous for a 17-year-old to drive in New York.

She came into therapy with Luke because she had caught him smoking marijuana in his room and learned that he'd also stopped attending classes in school. It became readily apparent that the family dynamic was a large part of the problem, and that his behavior reflected the dysfunction of his home environment—a rigid, controlling mother and a meek father, Jerry, who had emotionally checked out.

When I tried to explain the connection between controlling parents and rebellious children and attempted to teach Loretta that her rigidity was toxic to her sons' development and directly contributed to Luke's defiant behavior, she resolutely refused to acknowledge any contribution on her part or to modify her behavior in any manner. She actually said, "Look, I'm here for you to fix Luke, not me."

Okay, well, that's helpful...

Needless to say, my therapy with Luke didn't go far, because we could not address the root of the problem. Loretta's intransigent rigidity was a serious impediment to any progress because Luke's defiance was clearly a result of her inability to be attuned to his legitimate need for a natural transition to more autonomy. Her inability to adjust to changing circumstances, and to be more flexible in how she dealt with her family had greatly contributed to Luke's oppositional behavior, and without her changing, I found it difficult to get him to collaborate with the therapeutic process. To him, there was no point in dealing with his mother. However, he did come to understand that attending classes was the route to graduating from high school and leaving town to go to college, where he could be more independent at last.

CHAPTER 16

FACTOR ELEVEN: Active vs. Passive

Active

If you are genuinely motivated to change, you need to be an active participant in the process. That means investing the energy, drive, and initiative to work diligently toward your desired objectives. Active people schedule appointments, develop goals, and complete the assignments that they commit to with those goals in mind. They don't wait for someone to push them to work on themselves; rather, they are self-driven and push themselves to work toward the changes they set out to accomplish.

Active people live with a sense of purpose that drives them to do whatever it takes to achieve their important goals. They are proactive, and they don't wait until they are told to do something about the changes they need. They figure it out on their own—sometimes with therapeutic help—and then they do it.

Even if they don't realize what they need to do to achieve

a particular goal for change, once they discuss and agree to recommendations about how to work on their goals, they follow through and actively pursue them by doing whatever is required of them. They don't have to be held accountable for meeting their commitments because they hold themselves accountable without being reminded or pushed.

Active people are more likely to have a higher CQ than passive people because they tend to be more motivated, compliant, and intentional—all key components that quantify one's ability to change. They are usually highly motivated in general, and they don't wait for other people or external circumstances to drive them to work on themselves. They are compliant with agreed-upon instructions because active people get things done, that is, they do what is necessary to get things done. They are also usually highly intentional and focused on what they are trying to achieve to better themselves, without allowing themselves to get complacent or lazy.

Finally, active people don't rest on their laurels and stop moving ahead once they feel satisfied with what they have accomplished. For the sake of self-improvement, they constantly strive to accomplish the next step in their therapy or their careers. For them, life is a continually evolving set of goals they need to accomplish to become the best possible versions of themselves or to help others or improve the world.

Active people keep working on themselves. They embrace a continual journey of self-improvement and self-actualization.

Over the years, I have worked with quite a number of patients who, once they achieved their initial therapeutic goals, chose to continue therapy so they could keep improving themselves by developing new goals that promote greater growth and improved well-being.

These highly motivated, active individuals, who are not complacent about merely achieving their therapeutic goals, strove to attain the ultimate goal of self actualization. Their active nature allowed them to continue to develop themselves into the people they ultimately wanted to become, which invariably contributed to a high CQ.

Passive

People who are passive tend to be complacent and lacking self-direction. They don't initiate. They let others direct them to do what they need to do in order to change. They expect others to take the lead on projects, even with regard to their personal need to change, and they need others to hold them accountable, instead of holding themselves accountable in a reasonable, mature manner. Passive people don't usually feel that they have the agency to face life's challenges on their own. Instead, they rely on the people in their lives to tell them what to do and to guide them toward change.

Passive people often have dependent personalities and rely on others to motivate them, rather than motivating themselves. They wait to be told what to do, how to do it, and when, as opposed to figuring it out on their own.

I often find that passive patients grew up in controlling, dominating families, in which they were told what to do. They often were micromanaged to such a great extent that they had no opportunity for self-direction or initiative. Parents with controlling or obsessive-compulsive personalities often end up with passive children whom they've conditioned to expect to be told what to do and never to take independent action.

I personally find it quite frustrating to have a patient who sits in the office and just shrugs his or her shoulders when asked why they've come to therapy. Usually, they are present at the behest of a significant other in their lives, not of their own volition. Passive patients rarely, if ever, initiate discussions or develop their own goals. Instead, they come in with the goals that other people have decided that they need to work on. Passive people are often non-compliant with therapeutic assignments because they fail to recognize that the need to change requires active work toward specific goals. Generally, they prefer to sit and just answer questions passively, instead of initiating discussions by asking questions to gain self-knowledge or improvement.

Passive people often end up with a low CQ because of their difficulties with the factors that contribute to CQ, such as motivation, compliance, and intention. Too often, their motivation to change is low, precisely because accomplishing challenging goals requires active effort. They are often non-compliant because passivity can lead to avoidance or procras-tination. And they are rarely intentional, because working on your intentions requires the initiative and drive that passive people often lack.

CASE STUDY #14: SHERRY

Sherry came into my office after her parents reached out to me because they were concerned that she was "stuck" in her life. She was in her mid-30s and hadn't accomplished anything other than taking care of her three cats, which lived with her in her small apartment. She never finished high school because, in her words, she "didn't feel the need to finish because my grandfather left me a trust fund" that apparently could sustain her indefinitely. She didn't initiate much of anything. In fact, other than watching Netflix movies and going grocery shopping, she didn't do much of anything substantive.

Sherry was actually rather content with her limited life, and she preferred not to work on becoming more active or assertive, even on her own behalf.

It was obvious to me when I talked to her parents that they were driven, controlling people. They were both high-profile attorneys who worked together in their family law practice and had taken an active role in raising their children their own way. Their oldest son, who worked with them, had also become an aggressive attorney. Their younger son, who had a history of anger management issues and drug abuse, had been through a series of rehabilitation facilities and recovery programs. Their three children had very different reactions to their parents' controlling personalities: Their older son emulated them; their younger son reacted with rebellion, addiction, and defiance; and their daughter became my very passive patient.

Therapy with Sherry was challenging, to say the least. Her passivity became a roadblock for us because she expected me to be the only active participant and to direct every aspect of treatment, remind her of her assignments, and even help her formulate a goal for herself, since she could not come up with one on her own. She showed up regularly for her appointments, but she never initiated a comment or asked a question, choosing instead to sit quietly and wait for me to lead the session.

She obviously had been conditioned to be directed and controlled to the extent that she couldn't be an active participant at any level. Even though she tried to complete homework assignments, she failed to internalize them or apply them toward the goal of becoming a more active, self-initiating adult. She was developmentally stuck as a passive, complacent, 30-something functional adolescent.

Sherry's extreme passivity affected her ability to progress in therapy. She lacked the drive to put forth meaningful effort and actively pursue the goal of being more self-directed and goal-oriented. Her complacency was too strongly conditioned by her upbringing and too deeply embedded in her personality. It clearly undermined her drive to change. After a few months, we both came to the conclusion that she just didn't have the ability to be active enough to change herself or her life. She terminated therapy unceremoniously by sending me a brief text saying that she felt that she needed "a break" from therapy. Unfortunately, that break never ended, and I never heard from her again.

FACTOR TWELVE:
Disciplined vs. Uncontrolled

Disciplined

To accomplish the goal of substantive change and see the process through to completion, you have to possess a great deal of discipline. The Cambridge dictionary defines discipline as "the ability to behave in a very controlled way." This applies quite strongly to the change process for several reasons. First, as previously mentioned, the process of change is a marathon, not a sprint. You need a lot of staying power to get to the finish line. Sticking to the process and focusing on the end goal requires a lot of self-control—or discipline.

Second, being consistent in the process of change requires the discipline to keep therapy appointments, follow through with therapy assignments, and ignore distractions that can make you veer off course. People are far more likely to succeed in their change goals if they are disciplined and maintain their commitments. Self-disciplined people don't make excuses for not keeping their promises. Instead, they do what they commit to doing, regardless of what comes up or whatever distractions they may encounter.

The ability to change your patterns of unhealthy thinking, damaging emotional reactions, and maladaptive behaviors does require grit and determination. Changing dysfunctional patterns isn't easy; to do so, you must have the discipline not to give in to old patterns of thinking, reacting, and behaving. You almost have to be your own coach and hold yourself accountable to sticking to your commitment to change, not only at the macro level, but also—and perhaps more important—at a micro level. You need discipline to consciously prompt yourself, in the moment, to alter your patterns, brace yourself against your impulses, and not allow yourself to revert to old, damaging way of doing things.

To use sports as a parallel, for athletes to accomplish their goal of being successful stars in their field, they have to be extremely disciplined about training, practice, and execution. Imagine the discipline it takes for an Olympic ice skater, swimmer, or gymnast to get to the point of even making it into the Olympics, much less earning a medal. It takes years of daily and sometimes grueling practice to get to that point of athletic accomplishment. The people who succeed are extremely determined and laser-focused on accomplishing their goal.

This fierce determination and discipline are akin to what you need to accomplish your goals, as well. In my experience as a clinician, I can tell you with complete confidence that there is a strong correlation between self-discipline and therapeutic outcomes. The patients who were absolutely committed to working on themselves were much more likely to succeed in meeting their therapeutic goals than those who lacked the discipline to do so. That means they demonstrated the discipline to follow through on every assignment and worked hard to control their problematic thoughts, emotions, and behaviors.

This issue of discipline provides an example of how being somewhere on the healthier part of the Obsessive-Compulsive Personality Disorder (OCPD) can actually be a plus for someone who wants to change. People who have OCPD are far more likely to be organized in working on their goals and completing tasks. They actually tend to be uncomfortable when they don't do what they've committed to doing, so they are much more likely to complete their assignments and follow through on their commitments.

Many of my colleagues agree with me that they love working with people on the OCPD spectrum because they know these patients are more likely to keep their appointments and complete their assignments (and even pay on time!). In fact, a close colleague of mine who is transitioning toward retirement recently confessed to me that she is beginning to restrict her practice only to patients with OCD, "because they are the easiest to work with, and I don't have the wherewithal anymore to deal with the tough ones." She also admitted, "That's why I send those to you..."

So, if this description of a disciplined person fits you, this could contribute favorably to your CQ and may counterbalance against other factors stemming from personality features that are less conducive to change.

So, now let's examine the dynamics that contribute to a lack of discipline and how this deficit can make it difficult to execute real change and, subsequently, lead to a lower score on the CQ scale.

Uncontrolled

Disciplined people have the ability to control themselves. They can be deliberate in their behavior and make decisions in their best interest in terms of accomplishing their goals. Their self-control enables them to stay focused on these goals and to follow through on whatever it takes to achieve them. They also have the maturity to choose to do what they need to do instead of giving in to what they want to do, especially when the stakes are high.

In contrast, people who are uncontrolled lack the discipline to follow through on much of anything, unless, of course, it's something that interests them or meets their need for immediate gratification. They have great difficulty in completing tasks that require diligence or self-control without allowing themselves to be distracted or losing interest. For them, being compliant with requests or expectations is more of a chore or a bother, not the means to an important self-selected goal. As a result of their lack of discipline, people who have difficulty controlling themselves often can't accomplish what they set out to achieve. Teachers and colleagues often describe them as underachievers or underperformers.

This also applies to the issue of personal change as a goal. Uncontrolled people often lack the ability to exert the sustained effort to achieve any goals that require them to change something about themselves. They are either unable to keep up with what is required, or they aren't invested enough in their change goal because they know that achieving it will require a lot of discipline, which they know they lack.

People who recognize that they lack self-control most often find the entire process of change too daunting to undertake, or they can't muster enough discipline or even interest to sustain the effort that is required to achieve meaningful change.

A lack of self-control can stem from several different clinical issues. For example, people with Attention Deficit Disorder (ADD) often don't have good judgment and are too impulsive to exercise the self-control needed to achieve real change. Their brain—specifically the frontal lobe, which regulates executive functions such as impulse control, judgment, and task completion—is impaired to the extent that it compromises their ability to achieve any complex goal, unless they are very motivated. Otherwise, patients with ADD are often woefully unable to get things done or to work on making the changes necessary to function optimally.

People with Obsessive Compulsive Disorder (OCD) are also compromised in terms of self-control, except instead of being impulsive and acting without thinking about the consequences, they are more compulsive, and often can't control their thoughts (obsessions) or behaviors (compulsions).

In contrast to people with ADD, who don't stop to think about the consequences of their actions, people with OCD can't stop thinking or reacting compulsively. It's just beyond their control. Unless these unfortunate people can find ways through therapy to cope with this condition, life can become an endless sequence of uncontrollable experiences that render them hopelessly incapable of changing their very challenging circumstances. Narcissistic people also have difficulty controlling themselves because of their sense of entitlement. For them, rules don't apply. They come to believe they can justify their unhealthy or exploitive behavior because they convince themselves that they should be able to get whatever they want, regardless of who they hurt or take advantage of in the process.

Even more so, sociopaths—who do not care about the difference between right and wrong—have severe difficulty controlling their impulses to exploit vulnerable people for their own benefit. Conventional wisdom indicates that these people are very difficult to treat since they have little incentive or ability to change.

People diagnosed with Bipolar Disorder (Manic-Depressive illness) also have great difficulty controlling their behavior. They are intrinsically unstable and can quickly decompensate and lose control of themselves. When they get manic, they have no ability to exercise self-control, and they can deteriorate into an unmanageable state without any way to govern their behaviors.

Frequently, schizophrenics also have no ability to control themselves due to the psychosis that afflicts them. Their lives are sadly an endless series of breakdowns that limit their ability to achieve any meaningful change. With both Bipolar Disorder and schizophrenic patients, the usual therapeutic goal is to just maintain stability and not to achieve any degree of change.

People with these diagnoses often have a low CQ because they simply cannot control themselves, which severely limits their ability to sustain the efforts required for any degree of real change. Unless they can deal effectively with their underlying pathology—generally through intensive therapy and medication—the chances of successful change are quite low, which unfortunately translates into a lower CQ.

CASE STUDY #15: JACKSON

An energetic, charismatic 30-year-old, Jackson came to my office bursting with energy and charm, even though he was seeking treatment because his wife, Jennifer, had threatened him with divorce. She could no longer tolerate his lack of responsibility and his insensitivity toward her legitimate need for some semblance of order and predictability at home. He often slept late, never helped getting the children up and ready for school, and rarely followed through with anything she asked him to do, such as help around the house.

He was also struggling in his corporate real estate career due to his lack of structure and organizational skills, which kept him from managing his responsibilities. He worked for his father, who had threatened to fire him numerous times if he didn't get some sort of help to get his act together. However, having access to his family's considerable wealth, Jackson had little motivation to live up to his responsibilities.

He was diagnosed with ADHD in elementary school. His high degree of distractibility and poor impulse control led to frequent altercations with his fellow students. Although he was bright and tested with a high IQ, his behavioral challenges, disorganization, and inability to complete assignments limited his capacity to function academically.

Jackson also learned as a child that he could manipulate his weak, enabling mother to get whatever he wanted. Since his father was a workaholic who wasn't involved much with the family, he got away with behavior at home that other families normally would not allow without appropriate consequences. So, he really never learned much discipline, and between his ADHD and narcissism, he was a bit of a mess, both at home and at the office.

Trying to accomplish anything with Jackson in therapy was quite a challenge. He frequently came to sessions very late because he was distracted or simply didn't care enough to make the effort to arrive on time. He periodically skipped his appointments altogether and didn't bother to let me know that he wouldn't be attending. Getting Jackson to follow through on any homework assignments was futile since he virtually never bothered to accomplish anything between appointments.

At some point early in the therapy process, Jennifer discovered that he had gone to a strip club and engaged in sexual behaviors with one of the dancers. It soon became painfully apparent that he had a full-blown sex addiction, which had been going on for years with various such women, unbeknownst to his wife. Even this serious crisis in their marriage failed to move the needle to change his pattern of acting out. He persisted in his dalliances with club dancers, claiming that he needed a break from his nagging wife, who wouldn't engage with him sexually because she was too angry with him.

This pattern of gaslighting by distorting the reality of the situation, placing blame, and focusing on Jennifer's reactions to his poor behavior rather than dealing with his actions and the underlying causes that provoked her, only ended up alienating her even further.

When confronted with his resistance to stopping his destructive patterns of behavior, he admitted that he couldn't control the impulse to act out, and that he couldn't commit to following through with any homework assignments because he never remembered to do them and had too much going on to focus on them. He was also unable to be consistent with his ADHD medicine. He often forgot to take it and, as he later admitted to me, it made him feel dulled and too controlled.

His complete lack of discipline resulted in Jennifer filing for divorce. She had had enough of his abuse and failed attempts to change himself. At that point, he abruptly stopped therapy, claiming he felt that I was ineffective as a therapist because he "didn't get anywhere in therapy," so there was no point in continuing. He said he was going to get divorced anyway, and his time would be "better spent fighting her in court."

The combination of ADHD and narcissism kept Jackson hopelessly out of control and incapable of changing. When last I heard, he was still fighting with his father, who continued to threaten to fire him and cut him off, although they both knew that he never would.

CHAPTER 18

Factor Thirteen:
Optimistic vs. Pessimistic

Optimistic

The Oxford English Dictionary defines optimism as "hopefulness and confidence in the future or the successful outcome of something." The connection between optimism and changeability may not be readily apparent. However, if you look at optimism as thinking positively about your prospects of being able to change, then it's relatively easy to understand why being an optimistic person is highly correlated with CQ. If you are optimistic about your ability to change, then you obviously will be more motivated to work on yourself, because you feel that the outcome will be worth the effort.

Optimism also is highly correlated with traits that directly influence CQ. For example, studies show that it is highly correlated with a positive mood, good health, and motivation, all of which are essential ingredients in the ability to change. It just makes sense that if you are generally in a positive mood, in good health, and motivated, then you are more likely to work on things you feel you need to change.

A related concept, the expectancy effect, will help you understand the relationship between optimism and changeability. This effect suggests that if we believe that something positive will happen as a result of our efforts, that outcome is more likely to happen. This expectation of a positive outcome is a classic definition of optimism, and it can motivate you to work harder to change because you expect things to become better for you and those around you if you do the necessary work.

Optimistic people are also more likely to see that opportunities can arise in the future if they make efforts to change today. They are more able to envision a positive outcome and to see how that can change their lives and the lives of those around them. Because they are more likely to expect good things to happen as a result of their efforts, they are also more likely to be able to do the work required to change themselves into the person they (or their loved ones) want them to become.

Optimism is often inherited since personality features are often heritable, but it also can be learned. Cognitive therapy can be quite useful in identifying maladaptive thought patterns or cognitive distortions that influence the degree to which we can learn to be optimistic. Choosing to be around positive, optimistic people also can have a significant influence on our thinking and attitudes toward personal growth, but only if we allow that influence to happen. Being mindful about adopting a more positive attitude, being more optimistic in general, and observing how optimistic people think and view the world can be enormously helpful in becoming a more optimistic person and having a more positive attitude toward personal change.

Conversely, hanging around negative, pessimistic people can have a deleterious effect on your personality and attitude toward therapy and working on yourself in general. One warning: Being around people who have a negative attitude about therapy or personal growth can deepen your own pessimism about your ability or desire to change, so be careful who you select as your closest companions.

Now, let's take a closer look at pessimism and how it influences CQ.

Pessimistic

If optimism is strongly related to CQ, then conversely pessimism inhibits the ability to change. Pessimistic people are usually fundamentally negative. They assume that things won't work out in the end. They figure why bother trying to change if you are likely to fail? From their viewpoint, it actually makes sense not to invest in any efforts to change, since the outcome will probably be unsuccessful.

Pessimistic people tend to have had few, if any, positive experiences early in life. Their upbringing often did not include any incidents when they felt that they had succeeded or attained important goals. They may have had negative parenting experiences, with parents who were highly critical or who sent them such messages as, "You will never make it" or "Why bother trying—you are really a loser and you won't get anywhere in life anyway," or other variations on that theme. Children and young people internalize these messages and absorb the negativity inherent in that type of environment.

People who grow up in such homes, and experience negativity and/or traumas during their early developmental years, often end up developing a clinical disorder called *dysthymia*. It is essentially a chronic, subclinical depression that affects one's thinking, mood, behavior, and energy level. Dysthymic people are usually very negative in their thinking and expectations about their lives or about the world in general. Their mood tends to be rather dark, and their energy level is usually low. More importantly to our discussion, dysthymic people as a rule are generally pessimistic. They usually don't expect things to turn out well, and so they adopt a "what's the use?" attitude toward life in general.

As a result, it's generally difficult to motivate people who are dysthymic and pessimistic to do much of anything challenging, much less work on changing themselves. They are typically lethargic and have negative attitudes that inhibit their ability to see the value of making any effort to accomplish any goal since it is unlikely to amount to much.

The difference between dysthymia and depression, in the broadest of terms, is that people *get* depressed, but people *are* dysthymic. It's just how they developed, and it's their baseline way of functioning in life. In contrast, depression marks a dramatic change in a person's mood, thinking, and ability to function. People who get depressed exhibit marked changes that are obvious to those around them. They either sleep too much, or they have difficulty going to sleep or staying asleep.

They often change their patterns of eating, either eating minimally or overeating to soothe their depressed emotions. Depressed people can be suicidal, and their ability to function can be severely impaired. When people get depressed, they typically also become deeply pessimistic about themselves and their lives in general.

Dysthymic people can be otherwise fairly normal, function at an adequate level, and follow normal patterns of sleeping and eating. Their mood disturbance is usually more subtle and continual, without creating any marked change in how they function, emotionally or otherwise. They are simply negative people who don't expect anything positive in their lives or in the world in general.

Clinically depressed people have a limited ability to change because their thinking, mood, and behavior are significantly impaired. They lack the internal resources to function at any normative level, so when they are in a depressed state, their ability to work on themselves is usually quite minimal. Therefore, it is usually wise to make sure their depression receives vigorous treatment before they make attempts to change since depressed people typically have quite low changeability. Anti-depressant medication, cognitive behavioral therapy, activity therapy, and trauma therapy such as EMDR—if trauma is an underlying cause of the depression—can all be instrumental in preparing people to take on the challenges of working on themselves at a more general level.

Dysthymic people may be more difficult to treat and motivate to change. They are more "stuck" in their negativity and their pessimistic views of their changeability, Anti-depressant medication may be helpful, but dysthymia can be viewed as a depressive personality. It is a more ingrained way of functioning in general. Healing dysthymic people from earlier traumas and reprogramming the way they think, feel, and choose to show up in their daily lives most likely requires a more intensive therapeutic approach.

In my experience, people with dysthymia can change, but they have to be committed to the process of change and work on being more motivated to change themselves. This motivation is most often extrinsic because intrinsic motivation is usually quite low in dysthymic individuals. But, being motivated by a spouse who finds it difficult to be with such a negative, pessimistic person, or getting feedback from a boss about having a negative attitude, can be powerful engines in revving up someone's motivation to change.

The bottom line is, if you identify with either of the above descriptions, either of dysthymia or clinical depression, please get the professional help you need, whether from a psychiatrist who can provide medication or a psychologist or therapist for therapy, or most preferably, both. Research makes it abundantly clear that the combination of therapy and medication is far more effective in achieving a more positive mood and attitude toward your life or your ability to change than either alone.

CASE STUDY #16: RYAN

Ryan is a single man in his early 50s who grew up in an emotionally abusive home. His parents, Catherine and Kirk, argued and fought regularly, and then spilled their negative emotions over onto him. As an only child, he had no one with whom to discuss what was happening, and he felt trapped and alone for most of his childhood. His father, Kirk, especially targeted Ryan and frequently raged at him for not being academically motivated and for earning subpar grades. Kirk also resented Ryan for generally avoiding the family, but Ryan preferred to spend most of his time away from home with Jack, his one friend. Jack introduced Ryan to marijuana, which ended up being a daily escape for him, a habit that lasted for several decades.

Ryan had been sad and had suffered negative feelings about his life for as long as he could remember. His teachers described him as lazy and accused him of not putting forth any effort, but no one from school bothered to find out why or to inquire about what was going on at home. Ryan left home as soon as he could. He found a job in another state as soon as he finished high school and subsequently had little contact with his parents.

He came to therapy because he had a deep depressive episode that left him unable to leave his apartment or function at any meaningful level. It was apparent that depression had been a part of him for most of his life, at a more chronic, subclinical level, and that this current episode was a culmination of all of the negativity and loneliness in his life, which was inevitable at some point.

One obvious challenge was that Ryan had very little hope, after all these years, that he was capable of any change. He worried that he was too old, too broken, and too entrenched in his ways, which all fed into his negativity. Although hopelessness is—by itself—a symptom of depression, it seemed to be a more endemic part of his personality, leaving him generally sad and deeply pessimistic about his future and his ability to change his life.

When I asked Ryan about the possibility of taking medication to at least try to get the severity of the depression under control, he presented a flurry of reasons why medication hadn't worked for him, and why he wasn't willing to try it again. When I asked him about his previous experiences with therapy, he similarly listed all the reasons that therapy had not succeeded previously. I tried to explore ways to make this therapy experience different for him, but he replied honestly that he didn't think anything would help him.

However, a relative who understood Ryan's family dynamic had told him about the possibility of using EMDR to clear the baggage he was carrying, and he had promised her he would try it, although he really didn't think it would work for his hard-core depression and pessimism.

I could work with his willingness to try EMDR, but I had to be aware of the impact of the "expectancy effect." This is the cognitive bias that if you think something will work, it is more likely to produce a positive outcome, and conversely, if you are convinced it won't work, it's unlikely to move the needle at all.

Despite my efforts to increase Ryan's positive expectancy by getting him to read about EMDR and the underlying reasons for its powerful impact (it has a very high response rate, 75% to 80%), as well as to watch YouTube testimonial videos from people who described how EMDR changed their lives, Ryan's treatment was ineffective. His intense negativity about his prognosis and his general pervasive pessimism about the future led to the self-fulfilling prophecy that he couldn't do anything to improve his miserable life.

Shortly after our unsuccessful EMDR session, he texted me that he would not continue with therapy because there was no point in trying to work on himself when all of his efforts were clearly futile. He was convinced that he was a hopeless case.

FACTOR FOURTEEN:
Inquisitive vs. Defensive

Inquisitive

The road to changeability requires more than just being open. Openness is rather passive, like, "I'm open to hearing about it." Being highly able to change, however, requires a more active stance toward the need to change, including being willing to make the necessary effort. The word "inquisitive" better reflects a more active attempt to be curious, to inquire, and to search for solutions. Being inquisitive implies that you aren't comfortable with your current level of understanding or insight, and you want to pursue a deeper understanding of what ails you, or perhaps more often, what ails others about you.

Being inquisitive also means that you are a curious person. You don't just accept things as they are; instead, you attempt to comprehend things at a deeper level. You're prepared to figure things out so that you can have a better understanding. Curious people are usually quite growth-oriented; they are not complacent, or content to accept things as is. They ask questions and challenge the assumptions people make about things or about one another. Inquisitive people are more likely to work on themselves because they tend to be dissatisfied with the status quo in general, or with themselves in particular, and strive to do better.

Inquisitive people are rarely complacent. They wonder what they can do to improve their lives. They ask questions of themselves and strive to develop a more comprehensive understanding of what makes their personalities tick. This explains why being inquisitive factors into CQ and how important it is to ask questions about ourselves in order to derive a better understanding of our need to change.

Inquisitive people are not content to accept things as they are or to be complacent about information they receive. They don't interpret situations at a simplistic level, take information or events at face value, or interpret whatever happens to fit their own narrow narrative or agenda. They push themselves to achieve a deeper understanding and to appreciate the complexities of the situations they encounter, instead of settling for basic, black-and-white interpretations that keep onlookers in their comfort zone. Instead, inquisitive people are free to go beyond what is comfortable or convenient and to continue to process or analyze situations until they feel that they have a more accurate, comprehensive understanding that enables them to be more effective in dealing with situations as they arise.

Inquisitive people are indeed more open about things in general, and about themselves. This openness frees them to focus on self-improvement, growth, and self-actualization. It allows them to set goals and to think about what would help them function better or become a better person. Inquisitive people are open to receiving feedback about themselves and hearing how they can improve the way they live. And finally, they are freer to explore themselves, work on figuring themselves out, and determine how to change what they feel needs to change without problematic defenses getting in the way.

Defensive

The word *defense,* in Freudian terms, refers to mechanisms that people employ to protect their egos by defending them against threats that would compromise their stability or sense of self. We use defenses to maintain our self-image, the way we see ourselves.

Classic defenses that Freud described include denial, distortion, projection, repression, and rationalization. All of these defenses block our ability to be open and honest about ourselves. They keep us from facing uncomfortable truths about ourselves by deflecting or distorting reality so we can preserve our own narratives about ourselves or the situations in which we find ourselves.

By definition, defensive people are closed-minded and not open to hearing any perceptions or narratives other than their own. They tend to reflexively defend against any feedback they perceive as threatening to their fragile egos and to employ any of the above defenses to avoid facing the truth about themselves. Many defensive people come from highly critical families and developed their personalities as a result of the need to protect themselves from damage at the hands of their family of origin.

Defensive people are, by definition, not growth-oriented, and they are unlikely to change to improve themselves. Their primary goal is self-protection, which prevents them from experiencing the vulnerability that people need to feel in order to change and grow. The CQ of defensive people is typically quite low, because changing requires awareness of the need to change, which is usually low or non-existent in defensive people.

People who are defensive are also quite adept at projecting blame on everyone except themselves. Narcissistic people tend to project blame and also to be quite defensive and, therefore, they are more challenged in terms of CQ. Their closedness to what is wrong with them that needs to change is usually quite frustrating for their partners and is often the reason given when their relationships break apart.

One of the diagnostic criteria for Narcissistic Personality Disorder describes the inability to attain or sustain a mean-ingful or stable relationship for this reason, among others. Defensive people are typically ineffective in their relation-ships, often because they are closed to hearing anything that isn't aligned with their own narrative. It is difficult, if not impossible, to form a healthy attachment to someone who can't share another person's perspective and is blocked from even hearing anyone else's narrative. People who block out any input from other people that threatens their own perspective can't grow and usually have very low CQ.

I have often heard a spouse request—or plead—for a narcissistic partner to ask questions about what they are saying, instead of automatically arguing or defending their own position. The spouse is asking for his or her loved one to make the effort to show that they care enough about their partner to be inquisitive about what he or she is saying, especially if it contrasts with what the partner feels or claims to be true. These defensive partners fail to understand that *their* truth isn't necessarily *the* truth.

So, if defensiveness tends to be your interactive style, try to resist the urge or reflex to argue, take a deep breath, and think about what you need to know in order to understand where the other person is coming from, instead of trying to make your point. Try to stop, reflect, and be mindful of the need to inquire about what the other person is saying. This enables you to collect objective data that can help you analyze the situation from a different perspective, so you can reach common ground with the other person. This will lead to real growth on your part and will substantially increase your CQ.

CASE STUDY #17: RAYMOND

Raymond is a university student who came for treatment for pervasive anxiety and symptoms of OCD that were getting in the way of his academic success. His anxiety impaired his ability to focus and retain information. His OCD and indecisiveness made it difficult for him to complete exams on time and that consistently affected his test performance.

After I examined Raymond's background, it became apparent to me that a history of trauma throughout his earlier years had led to the development of his anxiety symptoms and that working on his trauma would be the treatment of choice. I gave him an assignment to read about EMDR and the effects of trauma on processing and memory. He carried out his assignment and came back with a list of questions about what he had read that demonstrated a clear need to understand EMDR and trauma treatment at a deeper level. He wasn't satisfied with just a cursory reading of the material; he wanted to be able to understand the concepts more fully and to know how they potentially applied to his situation. He also took the time to do his own research about the neurological effects of trauma on anxiety and how the OCD brain misfires when triggered.

Although this level of interest could be framed within the context of OCD (which would be a valid supposition), his inquisitiveness and need to take things to a different level of understanding enabled Raymond to develop a more complex comprehension of the work that we would be doing. As a result, it also helped him achieve a higher level of motivation.

His questions were probing and reflected his need for a deeper understanding that I felt would invariably lead to a greater and more sustained effort to achieve the changes he wished to make.

As a result of his intense desire to understand his particular struggles, and the resulting efforts to overcome his challenges, Raymond was systematically able to reduce the effects of his childhood trauma, desensitize the events that triggered his anxieties, and learn better coping skills. His academic performance improved so much that he graduated college magna cum laude and was accepted to a top law school.

CHAPTER 20

Factor Fifteen: Adequate Support vs. Doing It Alone

Adequate Support

Let's face it—changing yourself is hard. It takes honest self-appraisal, a commitment to do the work, and the perseverance to stick to your goals, even when the going gets tough. Having the right support when you are working on yourself will make the process less challenging, and more likely to succeed.

Why is support so necessary? For one thing, it helps to have someone who keeps you accountable for staying on track with your program. Many people use trainers or coaches to work on their fitness or life goals, even though they are perfectly capable of fulfilling those objectives on their own. They use these sources of support not only for the structure they provide and the encouragement they give, but also because people are much more likely to follow through on a task or a routine if they have to report their progress to someone who holds them accountable than they would be if they were on their own.

Having support also can mean having a therapist who, as discussed previously, can help set up a treatment plan that provides a clear path for achieving your goals. A good, organized therapist who can help you develop a structured plan and track your progress empirically toward measurable goals can give you valuable feedback that can help you maintain your motivation and drive.

Support can also come in the form of a diet or exercise partner who works with you to achieve similar goals in those areas. This person also can give you support when needed and can hold you to your end of the deal. If you know that you have committed to playing tennis twice a week with a partner, you are less likely to opt-out or make excuses not to follow through if you know that your tennis partner will be frustrated or disappointed if you don't show up.

Availing yourself of family support is often important in achieving a desired goal. Having someone in your family go with you to a therapy appointment or work with you on a specific assignment can make a huge difference in your ability to accomplish your goals. Similarly, joining a support group for people who have similar challenges, or a 12-step group for people with the same addiction, can provide an enormous source of support both when you are on track working toward your goals and when you get derailed and need a hand to help you get back on track.

This level of support contributes to CQ because you are more likely to succeed in changing yourself if you have support to keep you going when you struggle as well as having someone who will hold you accountable to follow through on your commitments. Having a team of supporters to cheer you on when you're working on yourself and to ensure that you are staying on track can make the difference between succeeding and failing.

Doing it Alone

Compared to the previous impediments to change that we have discussed, trying to change on your own is less black-and-white as a deterrent to change, and its success may depend on several factors. Generally speaking, trying to make a major personal change alone can be challenging because you are giving up the support and encouragement of those who care about you and can keep you focused on your goals. Not having anyone who will hold you accountable for your commitments can also lead to false starts and the inability to get where you want to be. Trying to do it alone is also more challenging because you won't have anyone objective or trained to help you to develop a plan of action, which—as we discussed in the previous chapter—can be an essential component of any change process, as well as CQ.

Additionally, the process of change can be long and drawn out, and you have to have the stamina and commitment to stick it out in the long run as you strive toward your desired goal. Trying to do this alone can challenge your ability to stay motivated, and may make an unsuccessful outcome more likely.

Instead, if you have the right support, you may be more likely to maintain your efforts over time due to a partner's encouragement and the accountability we discussed previously.

On the other hand, some people prefer to do things on their own, and they may actually be more likely to achieve their goals for change without involving anyone else. For example, those who are more independent-minded and accustomed to being self-sufficient may find that having someone else involved can be more of an irritant or a deterrent to the process. People who tend to be oppositional or defiant may also be more likely to resist change if someone tries to hold them accountable. But, when you leave them to their own devices, they can be quite successful in reaching their goals because they did it on their own without anyone telling them what to do.

Also, people who tend to be passive-aggressive, and who express their resentment by not doing what anyone asks of them—for instance, they may "forget" an assignment or an agreed-upon task as a way of showing their negativity—may actually be more successful in achieving some degree of success in changing themselves if there is no one involved to whom they can display passive-aggressive behavior. Left on their own, they are more likely to do what they need to do to change because their passive-aggressive dynamic has no context in which it can express itself. Embarking on the process of change alone may actually be an advantage for such people.

This analysis calls for reflection about your needs and what might help you or spur you to change. Do you tend to need the support of those who care about you? Would you do better if you involved someone who can provide structure and accountability to help you maintain your motivation for the effort of achieving your goals? Or, rather, are you an independent person who can organize and motivate yourself better on your own, doing things your way, instead of having someone tell you what to do and, thus, perhaps provoking you to resist and self-sabotage the very goals you wish to achieve?

Your effort to change this belongs to you, and it's up to you to think about it and decide.

SECTION III

Issues Related to CQ

"The secret of change is to focus all your energy not on fighting the old, but on building the new."

—Socrates

CHAPTER 21

How to Assess CQ

Assessing CQ

So, now that you are thoroughly schooled in everything (hopefully) that you need to know about changeability, let's pivot to a discussion about how to measure CQ.

Given the 15 factors that contribute to CQ, you can compute CQ by rating each factor simply on a range of 1 to 5, using the following scale:

1. Very Low

2. Below Average

3. Average

4. Above Average

5. Very High

If you are alone, then you'll need to rely on self-reporting information you believe to be true about how high (or low) you actually feel that you rank on each factor. It is important to try to be as objective and honest as possible in assessing yourself if you want an accurate report of your true CQ.

If you are in a relationship or have close friends who know you well and feel safe being totally honest with you, then first do your own self-assessment, and then choose your partner or a close friend—whoever you feel will be the most accurate—and ask them to rate you on all 15 factors. Then calculate the average of your score and the other person's score by adding them up and dividing by two.

You may also want to calculate the CQ of your spouse, partner, parent, or child. If that is the case, then try to be as objective as possible, and rate them on all of the factors as instructed above. This may be important in giving you a more reasonable idea of what you can realistically expect from them—if you are indeed expecting to see them achieve some changes.

So, after you have done the ratings, add up the scores of each factor, either yours alone or the average of yours and the other person's. The total score will range from 15 to 75. Here is the scale describing the range of CQ scores:

Level	Range	Likelihood of Change
1.	15–30	Unlikely to change
2.	31–45	Below to average probability of changing
3.	46–60	Average to above average probability of changing
4.	61–75	Likely to change

Level 1: 15–30

People who score in this range have demonstrated across the board that they don't possess the abilities required for meaningful change. They are generally not insightful or motivated and are just too limited to change. Ongoing expectations should reflect this reality; that is, you should not expect any real change to happen. This may seem absolute to you, but a person who scores in this range is unlikely to have the capacity to achieve meaningful change.

Level 2: 31–45

People in this range will have some difficulty changing, and you should moderate your expectations accordingly. However, if at least their motivation is higher, then significant and sustained effort to work on improving some other factors could possibly lead to some limited, but still meaningful, areas of change.

Level 3: 46–60

Those who score in this range are average to above average in their ability to change, and with the right motivation and effort, they should be able to demonstrate meaningful change in some areas, though they may be limited in others. Alternatively, they may be able to achieve modest gains in many or most areas, which would represent some overall improvement in their relationships or general functioning.

Level 4: 61–75

To achieve a score in this range, one must demonstrate significant strengths across the board in most or all areas that the various CQ factors measure, especially the crucial factors. People who score in this range are very likely to be able to demonstrate significant change in all of the areas they are targeting as treatment goals. They tend to be highly motivated, exert a tremendous degree of effort, and have significant strengths in most or all of the factors that make up CQ.

COMPUTING THE TOTAL CQ SCORE

Score each factor on a scale of 1 to 5.

Factor	Personal Score	Other's Score	Average Score
Motivated			
Trusting			
Workable			
Intentional			
Integrity			
Compliant			
Stable			
Introspective			
Analytical			
Flexible			
Active			
Disciplined			
Optimistic			
Inquisitive			
Adequate support			
TOTALS			

Total CQ Score divided by 15 _____

CHAPTER 22

How to Improve your CQ

Now that you have obtained a CQ score, whether for yourself or someone else, what can you do with this information? That depends on whether you are calculating a measurement for yourself or a loved one or, if you are a therapist, for your client.

For Yourself

First of all, congratulations for being bold enough to undergo this self-assessment. Just the fact that you are even interested enough in the concept of changeability to do this calculation says a lot about your inquisitiveness, desire to be introspective, and motivation to change. I think, therefore, that if you made the effort to read this book and took the time to do the self-report assessment to determine your CQ, it is unlikely that your score will be very low.

So, how can you best utilize the information about your CQ for your own growth and development? First of all, your overall score says a lot about your general capacity to change and how hard you'll have to work on yourself to achieve meaningful change. As we said earlier, if you were motivated to take the test, it is unlikely that your score is at the lowest level, Level 1, or "Unlikely to Change." Again, if you cared enough to read this book, you have at least some level of motivation or interest in the topic of change, and you're at least at Level 2, if not higher. Therefore, the level that your score represents is a good indication of how changeable you are overall and of how much work you would have to do to change.

If you are at Level 2, you will probably have a lot of work to do to be in the position to achieve the kind and degree of change you wish to accomplish. Accepting that reality is really the most important aspect of this process. It's meaningful to come to terms with the extent to which you will need to work on yourself to be more changeable.

If you are at Level 3, you are in a good position to make the changes that you want, but you are likely to face some areas that you will need to work on to maximize your chances for success.

If you are at Level 4, you are highly changeable, and you stand an excellent chance of achieving a positive outcome on your quest to change yourself.

What may be even more important than your level on the test is to examine the factor(s) in which you scored most poorly and to see what that means in terms of what could challenge your ability to change. Generally speaking, any score of 3 or below deserves some attention. The lower the score, the more likely it is that you will have to address that issue so you can remove it as an impediment to change. So, if you scored all 4s and 5s, and one 3, you want to work on that last factor to improve your ability to change. However, if you scored a wider range of scores, you first will need to attend mostly to those factors in which you scored the lowest.

So, what do you do with that information? I think that your best choice would be to develop corrective action plans for each of your lower-scoring factors. That means coming up with a few concrete ways to work specifically to improve in those areas. Using the following chart could be helpful:

To use it, place an "x" next to the factor(s) that you have identified as targets, then draft a corrective action plan for each one.

CORRECTIVE ACTION PLAN CHART

Factor	Score	Target Factor	Corrective Action Plans
Motivated			
Trusting			
Workable			
Intentional			
Having integrity			
Compliant			
Stable			
Introspective			
Analytical			
Flexible			
Active			
Disciplined			
Optimistic			
Inquisitive			
Adequate support			

To get a feel for how this can work, look at a sample completed chart:

Factor	Score	Target Factor	Corrective Action Plans
Motivated	4		
Trusting	4		
Workable	5		
Intentional	3	x	Work on goals, develop intentions
Having integrity	5		
Compliant	5		
Stable	4		
Introspective	2	x	Insight-oriented therapy Introspection skills training
Analytical	4		
Flexible	1	x	Target and reduce rigidity Explore ways to be more flexible
Active	4		
Disciplined	5		
Optimistic	3	x	Work on being more confident about achieving goal
Inquisitive	3	x	Prompt to ask questions Encourage to probe deeper

| Support | 2 | x | Talk to a friend about your goals |
| | | | Find a therapist to hold you accountable |

Total = 42 — Level 3 (*average to above average Ability to Change*)

Can you guess what type of person this could be, based on what was described earlier? If you guessed a person with Obsessive Compulsive Personality Disorder, you would be correct! People with this profile tend to be conscientious, motivated, and honest in their dealings with people. They make an effort. They also tend to work best on their own and to be self-directed, so they often don't have a high need for support or accountability. However, they tend to not be very insightful as to what they need to do to improve themselves, so they will need help developing concrete goals and broader intentions they can work toward to achieve the change that they seek.

People with OCPD also tend not to be very introspective and prefer to be task-oriented, rather than insightful. They like to accomplish things, instead of thinking about things, and they choose to stay in their comfort zone and avoid too much self-reflection. The corrective action plan would be to encourage and train the person to self-reflect, that is to ask himself or herself questions that would lead to introspection, such as: "What is getting in the way of my being more successful in my relationships?" or "What is preventing me from being happier in my life?"

And finally, as a rule, people with OCPD are usually rigid

in the way they think and behave. They have great difficulty being flexible. Helping them explore ways to be more flexible in how they think by presenting alternative ways of looking at a situation, or by offering them different responses to behaviors or reactions that aren't working for them, can help them become less rigid in their everyday lives and improve their relationships.

You can use the blank Corrective Action chart on page 133 to see which areas of CQ you need to focus on and to improve yourself. Please be honest and objective with yourself. If you asked your spouse or a trusted friend to give you feedback, incorporate their scores in the chart by using their numbers instead of yours. Their score is likely to be more objective and, therefore, more accurate. For any score of 3 or below, formulate at least two corrective action plans that you can work on to improve the factors you have identified as areas of weakness you wish to improve.

If you are working with a therapist, enlist his or her support in developing your corrective action plans, because it is likely that he or she will have a plethora of ideas you can draw from to choose plans that seem workable for you. If you're not working with a therapist (which you may want to consider doing), solicit opinions and suggestions from your spouse or trusted friend for possible ways to improve the areas of weakness that may affect your CQ. Researching the internet about these areas may also produce some ideas for working on yourself, as well.

Now that you have developed these corrective actions, the trick is to implement them to help facilitate the changes you wish to achieve. Whether you plan on doing this alone, or with the help of a therapist, identifying the areas that need improvement, having concrete plans designed to strengthen your areas of weakness, and implementing these plans in a structured manner will invariably help you achieve your goals of change.

Whether you are working alone or with a therapist, structure your plan to set aside time in your daily and weekly schedule devoted to implementing your corrective action plans. Unless you devote specific blocks of time to doing what you need to do to achieve your goals, the work is unlikely to happen because other things will always get in the way. So, once you have decided what your action plans are, set time aside in your calendar and stick to it!

For Family and Friends

If your goal in completing the CQ was to evaluate the changeability of someone in your life, be it your spouse, sibling, parent, or a child who is clearly having difficulties that also may be affecting you, then the results of the CQ may give you clarity as to how realistic your expectations are about how much this person can change. If the CQ is at Level 1, then you'll need to get past those expectations that your loved one will change, because, in all probability, he or she won't. It's just not going to happen, and I'm sorry if that sounds bleak. The CQ score indicates that this person is likely just too limited in too many areas to achieve significant change.

Before drawing any black-and-white conclusions, however,

it may be helpful to check the accuracy and objectivity of your scores by consulting with the person's therapist, if there is one involved, or with someone else who could objectively rate the scores. You can then compare your set of scores to check how objective and accurate they are.

If the person is at Level 2, you probably need to adjust your expectations way down, because the process of change will be challenging given the number of factors that will affect the person's ability to change. That doesn't mean that it won't happen, as in the case of Level 1, it just means that your loved one will have to buy into the CQ concept and look at what factors he or she needs to work on to maximize the possibility of a positive outcome. That may require sitting down with the person to explain the CQ process and gently ask if your ratings seem accurate.

Try to make a transition into a discussion of how to use CQ as discussed above to enhance the probability of success. Alternatively, you may want to try to bring your loved one into the process by collaboratively rating him or her together, and seeing how aligned or far apart you are in your ratings.

People who are in either Levels 3 or 4 are likely to have the motivation and the wherewithal to accomplish their goals, and you can choose to share the results with them, celebrate how high their CQ is, and encourage them—since they are so changeable—that their efforts to change are likely to be worthwhile. You can also use the CQ to assure yourself that change is probable to some degree, at least. Celebrate that your loved one is likely to achieve the goals of having a better life and becoming the person he or she wants to be.

Note for Therapists

If you are a therapist, CQ can be a useful tool for you to use to enlighten your clients about the utility of understanding their current degree of changeability and determining how to identify their potential areas of improvement. It will be especially helpful in assisting clients in developing concrete corrective action plans for working on improving their areas of weakness.

It can also be very helpful to include a spouse or significant other in the CQ process. On the one hand, if you are concerned about how limited the client seems to be, perhaps his or her CQ has been underestimated, and the person is more likely to be able to change than previously thought. Making this determination can be encouraging for a loved one who thinks that change is pretty much hopeless but who now can see the client's potential for change and be more optimistic.

Alternatively, it is also possible that loved ones may have unrealistic expectations of your client, and are, as a result, frustrated or resentful of the person's lack of progress toward therapeutic goals. Using CQ to help a family understand the real limitations impeding your client's ability to make more progress and have some empathy for his or her struggles could be very helpful for the entire family dynamic. Similarly, sharing and explaining the client's corrective action plans can give a family member real hope that this process can facilitate an improvement in the person's ability to achieve badly needed changes—a boost for the client and the family.

SECTION IV

Final Thoughts

"When we are no longer able to change a situation,
we are challenged to change ourselves."

—Viktor E. Frankl

Epilogue

Thank you for taking the time to read this book. My hope is that you will take away some of its ideas and learn from the case studies presented. Perhaps more importantly, I hope the use of the CQ as a tool to assess and improve your changeability or that of a loved one, or a client, will enhance your—and their—well-being and life satisfaction.

I often turn to my rich heritage of Jewish tradition for insight and inspiration. Even though the patients I treat run the gamut in terms of race, religion, and cultural background, somehow, they genuinely seem to appreciate words of wisdom from my Jewish background. So, I would like to close by sharing two ideas that I hope will give you some food for thought and perhaps some inspiration to consider the prospects of changing for the better and facilitating further personal growth.

First, the word "to change" in Hebrew is *leshanot*, which comes from the same root as the word *shana*, (as in Rosh Hashana—the Jewish new year), which refers to "time." So, what does change have to do with the concept of time? Well, as the adage says, "Time never stands still." In other words, time is not static; it is in a perpetual state of motion, always changing. The ideal way of living isn't staying static, or stuck, like a broken clock, but being constantly fluid, always looking for new opportunities to grow.

The study of the Torah, or the Five Books of Moses, never ends; as soon as we finish reading it, we immediately go back and read it again. The same is true with the Talmud—there is never an end game; it is a perpetual process of review and refinement of insights and understanding. In Judaism, one never finishes the study of Torah. We are constantly in a state of fluidity, always looking for new insights, a deeper understanding of what we have already learned, and new texts to delve into and explore. Similarly, an evolving person looks for new ideas and different ways to understand concepts that affect his or her self-development and personal growth.

And second, there is a famous Hebrew saying: *Im lo maalim, yordim*, which literally translates as, "If you don't go up, you go down." This refers to the concept that if you aren't growing and making the effort to work on yourself, to improve or change, you will inevitably regress. This confirms the ancient Jewish value of study and learning, because, without it, you can't grow. And if you don't grow, you won't change.

So, this axiom suggests that you can't ever let your guard down or be complacent or think that you've done enough. You can't rest on your laurels. Ideally, life should be a constant journey of self-exploration, always seeking new ways of thinking and of seeing the world and always looking for steps you can take to improve.

In real life, there is no graduation. Life is a continuous pursuit of new ways to change ourselves for the better.

Acknowledgments

My most valuable teachers have always been my patients. I have learned so much from their many insights and challenges. Over the years, they have inspired me with their grit and determination to become their authentic selves, who they would have been had they not been derailed by circumstances that were beyond their control. They have a truly remarkable ability to transform themselves through therapy, even though it is often arduous work. I will always be grateful to them for trusting me to be their agent of change.

I also am thankful for my equally remarkable (and interminably patient) editor, Erica Meyer Rauzin, who gently shaped the book toward its final version. Her gifted talent in balancing art and form has greatly contributed to my ability to complete this project.

Thanks also to Gary Rosenberg of The Book Couple for another superb publishing job. And thanks to Karen Zarkower, my tireless administrative assistant, for all she does to support all that I do.

I also want to thank my family for their undying support and encouragement.

About the Author

Originally from Newport News, Virginia, Dr. Norman Goldwasser is a clinical psychologist in Miami Beach, Florida. He earned Master's degrees in Clinical Psychology and Industrial-Organizational Psychology, and a Ph.D. in Clinical Psychology summa cum laude from the Virginia Commonwealth University in Richmond.

Trained as a cognitive-behavioral psychologist, his primary focus of treatment and writings has been in the field of trauma. He is widely regarded as an expert in Eye Movement Desensitization and Reprocessing (EMDR), having been a clinician, consultant, and trainer over the past 30 years.

He is an internationally known speaker on various topics including child sexual trauma, marital issues, educational psychology, positive psychology, and spirituality. He has consulted with more than 100 businesses, law and medical practices, hospitals, and educational institutions throughout his career. More recently, he has volunteered in Israel to treat trauma victims, soldiers, and their families and to train therapists to use EMDR.

Dr. Goldwasser's previous book, *Breaking the Mirror:*

Overcoming Narcissism—How to Conquer Self-Centeredness and Achieve Successful Relationships, has received much critical acclaim. In addition to *CQ: The Changeability Quotient,* he is completing his third book, *Mindful Prayer: A Clinical Approach to Achieving a Deeper Spiritual Connection,* which is set to be published shortly.

Dr. Goldwasser is most proud of his seven children, 28 wonderful grandchildren, and three amazing great-grandchildren.

www.ingramcontent.com/pod-product-compliance
Lightning Source LLC
Chambersburg PA
CBHW071741120626
46550CB00002B/615